RED

Lion

OF SALES

(Interestingly inspiring and richly
informative.)

MATHIAS MACHONA

Email: info@redlionofsales.com

Website: Redlionofsales.com

Tel: 07360159574

Mathias Machona Publishing

Flat 40 innis house east street SE 17 2JN

Email: info@redlionofsales.com

Tel: 07360159574

Synopsis

This is the story of my life about how I was homeless. But because I have a talent for singing, I wrote a few songs and went around London selling them, until I discovered the mystery of a customer's mind. So, I'm not penning down theory lessons taught by another teacher or philosopher, but documenting my own original knowledge and experience of selling products directly to one person at a time in the UK. Mostly from Westminster to Buckingham Palace, Mayfair to Knightsbridge, Knightsbridge to Soho, Leicester Square to Oxford Circus, London Bridge to Waterloo, City of London and many other places before people nicknamed me the Red Lion of Sales. Because I was so good at selling my product (music).

Introduction

In this inspiring book, you will learn the secrets and basics of how to make £60 a day, £300 a week and how to build a business out of it to become a millionaire selling any product or service. This money will feed you and cover all your living expenses like rent, food, transportation, weekly, monthly, yearly, and it will allow you to live the life of your dreams. So, I'm going to teach you how to set aside some money as capital for the business you want to start, starting with a small foundation. Jeff Bezos, the number one billionaire, said, big things start with small things, so I don't write theory lessons taught by another teacher or philosopher. But I am documenting my own experience of selling products directly to one person at a time in the UK, mainly in the City of London, Westminster to Buckingham Palace, Mayfair to Knightsbridge, Knightsbridge to Leicester Square, Leicester Square to Oxford Circus, Oxford Circus to London Bridge, London Bridge to Waterloo, and many other places before people nicknamed me the Red Lion of Sales. So follow me on this adventurous journey to learn and explore the little secrets of the customer's mind. Mathias Machona is a business author His vision is to sell any product or service until he reaches billionaire club status, training young and old entrepreneurs to become red lions like himself. He uses his skill to win sales until he reaches billionaire club status.

Contents

Chapter 1

My Short Biography

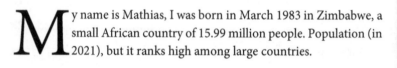

My name is Mathias, I was born in March 1983 in Zimbabwe, a small African country of 15.99 million people. Population (in 2021), but it ranks high among large countries.

My father worked as a driver for the United Nations. He left my mother for another woman when I was 2 days old. My mother fought hard to raise us as a single mother, me along with my half-brother and half-sister. I grew up in Harare, the capital city of Zimbabwe, in the Highfield district, an area called Egypt, under President Robert Mugabe.

The area I grew up in was a high density suburb with high poverty and high crime. I went to elementary school and then high school (college) until the fourth grade, but I dropped out last year, and started hanging out with bad guys who weren't interested in school.

How My Mother Struggled to Bring Me Up

As my father was working for the United Nations, my mother lived in the village with my grandmother along with my father's brothers and sisters, and my mother was often abused and beaten for no reason.

My Mother's picture

They overworked her in the fields and forced her to do housework like a slave. They just hated her for no reason, which is typical of African in-laws in numerous instances. Even my father would brutally beat her when he came to the village because his relatives influenced him.

There was a lot of domestic violence. I was not my parent's firstborn. Their first child died when he was 6-months-old because my grandmother was into witchcraft and also hated my mother. She killed the baby by bathing him in cold water, and he turned yellow. One day, when my mother's younger sister came to the village. She saw how terrible my mother's condition was. She was emaciated, she looked so worried and sad, you could tell she was not well at all. Therefore, when she returned to the city and told my grandfather, my father to my mother how my mother had been abused and how her health had deteriorated. With great anger and frustration, my grandfather and his wife went to the village to demand answers about what was happening to their daughter. Then everything came out about how my mother was beaten and abused, so my grandfather and his wife got furious and said they couldn't let them kill their daughter (my mother) so they told my mother to pack her bags to go away. They took her home to the city to live with her and said that if my father still wanted to be married to their daughter, he would follow her to the city to their home where he was unable to abuse her, so my father agreed. So, they went back to my grandfather's House number 2219 in Harare, Highfield, Egypt, the ghetto where I was born.

My Dad Is on the Left, Wearing a Maroon Shirt and Black Pants

Then my father and mother happily continued their marriage in the city. And I was born there when I was 2 days old, my father left my

4

mother and took another woman and got her pregnant. He also left her after she gave birth to a son and went to another woman again. Not only that, he continued to live this lifestyle and those women couldn't let him take care of me. They were the ones who ate his money. So, my mother had to take the responsibility of taking care of me. She sold wine, beer and later left the country to countries like South Africa, Mauritius, Botswana to buy clothes and wine and resell them to businessmen and businesswoman with shops back in Harare. All this to take care of me, then she had two more children from other relationships. My mother continued to take care of us, and when I finished in primary school, she sent me to a boarding school called St Francis of Assisi. I didn't do well in school. I was always the last (failed more than everyone) because I had a problem that was bothering me and preventing me from learning and studying. The problem was that I couldn't see the board when the teacher was writing and teaching on it, so I was left out. And I was unable to make it in my studies, and I entered St Francis of Assisi boarding School, not because I had the qualifications. But my uncle bribed a bright, intelligent boy to write the entrance exam for me as if I were him. And he passed, and when I went to boarding school and started failing the annual seasonal exams, some of the teachers became suspicious because I always failed, but it was too late for them to do anything. So, my constant failure left my mother no choice but to terminate my admission to that boarding school. She took me home and transferred me to a cheaper local high school, which I later dropped out to join the bad kids at my school who weren't interested in education. Nonetheless, before I left, I remember complaining to my mother one day that I couldn't see the blackboard at school. She listened and sent me to the opticians to get my eyes checked, the opticians confirmed that I needed glasses to see clearly. Then she bought me glasses and I could see very well. I was delighted, and I told all my friends that now I can see the writing board and the world more clearly, but over time my glasses got lost, but my mother never made sure that I always had those glasses. This was the reason why I failed in school and thanks to copying and cheating, I learned certain knowledge by copying the answers of other students in class. But in general, I am a smart and intelligent person with a high IQ, which is why I became an author who now writes business books without any education or degree, and educated people will learn from my books. College students, graduates, entrepreneurs, business women, presidents, queens, big and small, will learn from my business, knowledge and sales experience because I'm not stupid. But I'm intelligent.

My Future Plan to Help Children

I want to campaign for a law that requires all children starting primary school to have their vision tested to see whether they can see the writing board or not. They should be tested for short-sightedness or far-sightedness, the type of sight test. People do before getting a driving license, they need to test children's vision to help children who can't speak for themselves because I couldn't see the writing board clearly. But I was unable to tell my mum because she was always busy taking care of us, but she never bothered to ask me or find out why I'm not doing well in school with academics. I needed glasses to improve my vision and help me see the board clearly, and so are many kids who are not doing well in school today. It's not because they're not good at academics, it's because their eyesight isn't good enough to see the board when the teacher is teaching them, and because they can't talk for themselves, they just shut up, hoping their parents will care. And be responsible, but their parents don't see that their children need glasses at school. Therefore, a law should be passed to help children get their vision checked before they enter primary school, so that if they need glasses, they can be provided with these glasses to help them learn and ensure a good future. In addition, a record of children requiring glasses should be kept on file so that they are required to have those glasses before attending classes during their apprenticeship career. And parents should be held responsible for the well-being of their children.

Coming to England

When I was 17 years old, I came to England with my uncle and started living here in the UK. I did all sorts of jobs that every African does before settling down. My first job was in building construction. I worked as a laborer in Surbiton near Kingston upon Thames, and then I got a job as a live-in carer. I was making good money, I was doing well, but I lost my job because of a problem. A disabled client I cared for approached the management of the care agency I worked for and accused me of theft. He said he sent me to the store to buy something and I came back with the wrong change, and I was £1.50 short of completing the correct change I should have given him, so the live-in care agency suspended me for these charges until further notice. And the matter had to be resolved before I could start working again, so I ran out of money to pay the rent and other bills, therefore I gave up and started living homeless.

My Days in Homeless Day Centres

Homeless people used to gather in Deptford reach SE8, and we had a free meal, breakfast, everyone could have as much toast and tea as they wanted, so there were many people with big bellies because of eating too much toast bread and drinking tea. People sat and chatted all day with all sorts of people who were hopeless drug addicts, divorced, depressed, thieves, ex criminals, and the place stank because some people didn't want to bathe, but the showers were there they were people who could wash if they wanted, and everyone had free clothes, so I showered there and got my used clothes there.

The Rats Eat My Meal

In my homeless days, before I started selling CDs, I begged like many beggars on the street, standing aside the road begging for 5p, 1p, 2p, 50p to find money to buy a dinner like chicken and chips and I remember one day when I begged all day and collected a few pennies on the floor until I found 2 pounds and after buying chicken and chips I went to the church, the building I stayed in as a homeless person, but when I left my chicken and chips hidden behind some chairs in a dark alley where there was no light. I went upstairs to attend the service that was going on upstairs and when I came back I was so hungry and waiting for my chicken and chips for the day but when I came back, all I saw was an empty box of chicken and chips with holes everywhere. I was very disappointed and said the rats ate my chicken and chips. I am starving because I expected to eat the chicken and chips, but the rats stole my food. So, these are things that I will never forget when I lived as a homeless person. It was fun. I will never forget this story, and when the rats ate my food, I had to beg for money again to get something to eat, but that night I slept hungry because I couldn't find anyone to give me money. Life in the UK wasn't easy for me when I was homeless, sleeping on the floor of a church building with rats or mice crawling on the floor, howling at night, sleeping with cardboard boxes on the cold floor when it was freezing. I slept and lived in the church I remember

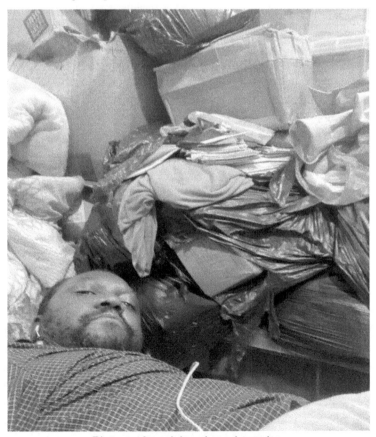

Picture of me lying down homeless

During my homeless days, I used to go to the city at night and sleep outside some buildings built around Leicester Square and some cinemas in their courtyards. Sometimes some restaurants close down and beggars and squatters use them as a place to sleep, so I put some boxes of papers, and I slept on the floor on the boxes of papers, and I slept in the cold and rain many nights, many days, many months, many years with other homeless people, we slept on the floor and packed up in the morning. And come back at night I used to sleep on the floor in Soho and sometimes drunks would pass by where I sleep and pee next to me. Then I'll scream stop peeing don't you see I'm sleeping here, and drunks will say oh sorry, and would walk away, and sometimes I would go to McDonald's and sleep at the tables and sit with other homeless people in the open McDonald's on Walworth road near the elephant and castle, many nights I would sleep there because there was no guard there to chase us away. Sometimes I would sleep on the buses from where they would start their journey to their final destination until the bus drivers got tired of me and often got me to get off the bus, so I had a rough time of my life. I have struggled with so many struggles, but my ambition to achieve something in life one day and to come out of poverty kept me going, my ambition kept me focused.

A Thief Stole My Nike Shoe While I Slept

During my time of homelessness, I recollect a day when I was situated in Leicester Square. I arranged my cardboard boxes on the ground and settled down for the night. Later, I headed to McDonald's and ordered a hot chocolate. After removing my Nike trainers, I placed them beside me and went to sleep. However, upon waking up the next morning, I discovered that my Nike shoes were missing, and it was pouring rain outside. I realized that a thief had taken advantage of me while I slept, as the area was notorious for drug users and burglars who would steal anything they could get their hands on. Feeling embarrassed and ashamed, I sat on the wet ground with bare feet. I remembered that I had £10 in my pocket and decided to search for a nearby Primark store, where I could purchase inexpensive shoes. After spending my money wisely, I learned that even second-hand shoes can be stolen by thieves while we sleep. This experience was a reminder of my struggles in my homeless days.

The Sad Story of My Homeless Friend, a Former CEO and Millionaire

One day at the homeless day center, while we were standing in line for sandwiches to get tea for breakfast, I made friends with a 50-year-old man who was once a rich man worth 15 million pounds in the United Kingdom. He was one of the pioneers of ringtones, innovating and selling ringtones However, two shareholders of his company wanted to sell the company, but he personally did not want to sell the company. He wanted to realize its full potential, but for another reason he had to compromise and sell the company. And they sold the company for £30,000,000 and he himself got a bigger stake, he got £15 million. But overtime this once rich man worth 15 million squandered all his money until he was broke and, as we speak, is now a beggar, homeless and now standing in line for free sandwiches. He told me how he spent his money, he said, he used to buy £400,000 worth of bottles of wine to drink with his girlfriends. Furthermore, he once showed me receipts from a restaurant he went to with another model, and they charged him £450,000 just for a bottle of wine. He told me he had all the girls he wanted, he was always in hotels with models, this man wasted all his money on women and other useless things until now he is broke and homeless. And this is a lesson for the rich man. You should know that if you are working to earn money, remember to invest it in activities that will earn you more money. Don't be stupid with your money because money is like a bird, it has wings. If you don't put it in a cage it will fly away, so be smart. You can go as high in the sky as the high and mighty on earth, but you can also go down further if you are not careful, save money. Invest in assets that would give you three times as much in your lifetime, even in retirement. But sad for my former millionaire friend who squandered his fortune only to be begging.

I Have Been Through the UK Benefits System

Not having papers contributed to my being homeless. I remember when I lost my job, I couldn't claim unemployment benefits because I didn't have indefinite leave to live in the UK, but I was an illegal immigrant but over time I got my papers and got out of homelessness, but something odd happened and I didn't get my benefits because I was late on the day I was supposed to sign, so they couldn't take it, and they stopped the benefits, so I became homeless again for a long time. And I was unable to receive my benefits from the UK benefits system.

How I Tried So Hard

So, as I said in the previous paragraphs, I am a person who has worked hard to earn money, often, like anyone else, I tried to get by in a normal job, at work I tried to please my bosses, but no matter how hard I tried, I wasn't accepted because I was unlucky. I tried to work as hard as everyone else to get promoted, I tried to be smart, but it didn't work because I was always dismissed for not being good enough. So, I looked for work until I got a job as a cameraman, a TV cameraman for a charity which paid me £200 a week, and I was doing well until I was promoted to head of that TV channel that was broadcasting on Sky TV. So, I worked all kinds of jobs in different workplaces like cleaning, warehouse, restaurants, but it's only when I decided to stop being a slave working for people and being paid peanut, that I started to sell something as a product, my music CD with songs I wrote because I like to sing. I started selling my music.

Picture of my music CD

From a modest £1, I raised the price to £2, gradually the price became £5.00 per CD of 4 tracks, then I discovered this special system and formula that works perfectly for anyone selling any product or service!

My Songs

So, I started selling my raw a cappella songs that I wrote and brainstormed on my phone recorder and put them on a CD on my computer using Windows Media Player. I sing upbeat (happy) soul music, the 4 song titles I sold were (a) Tough Girl (b) Sunny Day (c) How Beautiful You Are (d) So Far Away. First I went to a client (customer) with a pitch or a story I had worked on and it started with, Hi, my name is Mathias, I'm selling music single for £1, are you Interested? Some clients said no, others said yes and gave me money for my product. And here are the secrets I discovered about how to sell a product, which I will share with you in more detail in this book.

There Are Three Kinds of Customers When It Comes to Selling a Product or Service.

The First Customer

A customer who will listen to your presentation or offer, look you in the eye and nod at everything you say with a smile on his face and gives you money in exchange for your product and sometimes ask for a first time buying experience only to try or taste your product before buying. This customer is a green light at a traffic light.

The reason they buy the product is:

-You stir their emotions, which encourages them to buy from you

-They need your product because it's good for them

-They just want your product, even though they may not need it

- They are moved by the way you present yourself to them with charisma

-Your friendly smile and sincerity, excitement, or maybe you're just funny

-Your professionalism

Second Customer

The Undecided Customer 50/50

A customer who wants to buy but doesn't want to buy, is interested in your product but doesn't buy, so they will listen to you from the moment you approach them and if you give them your word (offer), they also Ask you about the experience or taste of your product, and when you're done, they will smile at you and say, no, thanks, or they'll make excuses like they don't have money, they just pay by card, or whatever, and other excuses for saying no, and those types of customers are like an amber-orange traffic light.

Third Customer

The third customer is a rude customer. They just tell you to leave, or give you a sign to leave, or a facial expression. They don't even want to see you or talk to you, and this type of customer is like a red light. These are the three types of clients I have seen making £60 a day, £300 a week, an average of 72 sales a week. I sell 12 products a day for £5.00.

CHAPTER 2

Customers Are Numbers

T he Numbers Game

I will break the math to earn £60.00 a day £300 a week

1-You need to create a presentation or story (pitch) about your product

2-The first goal should be to sell 12 products per day to customers

3-Kindly approach 2000 people per day, 14000 people per week

This is the math that will earn you £300 a week if you sell your service or product for £5.00 And you can use this math to sell any product for any amount. You must have the temperament of a lion. When a lion is hungry He goes hunting in the wild or in the forest, girded with his ability to kill and his instinct to kill, when he sees his prey, he attacks and catches and eats it Sometimes he catches small, sometimes big prey, but he will always be full and have enough to eat because he understands that food is not thrown into his mouth from heaven, but that he has to go hunting, looking for food to eat and feed his family. Similarly, as a salesperson, you need to understand this principle and have the character of a lion to succeed in this sales game and build a sales business. With the ability to work hard intellectually, find customers who will buy your product, even if it means traversing the community, the country, and the world to find customers willing to give money for your product. So, for you to have the lion character to have the opportunity to constantly travel the world searching for prey, you must always remember the basics of selling, remember that the lion character is the king of the jungle. So, you take your product or service, and you go out and ask everyone if they want your product, and you will find numerous customers who are interested in your product, and before you know it you'll be making hundreds, thousands and millions of sales.

Red Lion

Before going hunting, the lion is driven and courageous. He has a drive, a hunger, a roar, a determination, so if you have the attitude of a lion, you will be successful with what you sell. You will be the king in the sales game, the king in your country and the king in the world. If you don't develop these lion skills, you will not achieve anything in this game, so learn from the Lion's character, skills and abilities. Lions dominate their environment, so train yourself to have these qualities and be strong. For example, Steve Jobs, the founder of Apple, was a business-savvy person who was determined, courageous and driven to succeed. He had a vision to distribute his Mackintosh computer to businessmen and ordinary people all over the world, and he succeeded. His product is the most expensive selling product and his company is the most valuable company on earth, so learn how to plan, and start selling your product to your customers, get paid and get rich! Be hungry as a salesperson, be motivated, be determined, be brave.

Stop Thinking About Money

It's good if you're out and about or during sales to go for short breaks because when you start thinking about money, you fail to sell you will be disappointed it will spoil your attitude, so it is always better to focus on your actions like a smile, have a lot of energy and have fun selling your product or service because selling is very fun for me personally I like it, and I am happy, especially when I get a customer's attention, and they look me in the eye, we connect, and they are convinced to buy my product after our conversation it means everything to me, so it is important to focus on the product that is in stock instead of thinking about your budget or profit. For example, let's say you have 40 products in stock, you have to focus on making and selling them until they get down to 30, and when they get to 20, you have to focus on 20 you work every hour until they get to 5, then to 0 and you sell out. Don't look at the money or how much you've earned, don't look at the budget you have to reach because it will make you work harder doing 2 things at the same time. Don't look at what you have to get and save, focus on the work, money should be the last thing on your mind, but you can count your money at the end of the day. That's why it's called daily production, this is done at the end of the day when you calculate your losses and winnings.

System & Time

Don't take your business personally because if people don't buy your product, it has nothing to do with what your face looks like, it has nothing to do with your ethnicity, whether you're African, Asian, American or European or whatever race. Business is not personal, it's not about a bad day or a bad year that you don't sell, no, every day is a good day, and you're a good person, selling a product is all about knowing the basics, a system that works with the time it takes to apply them, so they can provide the best daily, weekly, monthly and yearly average sales income. I call system and time sales twins because they work together if you know your average production volumes, if you work 8 hours a day 6 days a week and if you know how many people you need to talk to or how many customers you need to get to earn an average of £60 a day. So business is not personal, never take things personally by saying people don't like me or this person is not a good person because they refuse to buy my product or the services I offer them no! Business is a system that works over time. Knowing the system, knowing how people agree to buy your product, learning that the system is like a clock that has a system that shows the time from noon to noon and repeats the same system 24 hours a day, 7 days.

Weekly, monthly and 365 days a year, the same process repeats itself over and over again So learn the system, know the system and work the system and time to sell your product, expect your average sales production and build your business, then never feel bad or tell yourself that you are the guilty person or that you are wrong. Just execute. What is a System? Implies how something works or a pattern, repetition or way of doing something.

Work Your Full 8 Hours

The product is sold at different times of the day, sometimes at the start of your business hours You sell, sell, sell, even before the end of the day you have sold enough to meet your average daily sales that occurs when I sell my product, sometimes I sell from the beginning of the day. I sell, sell, sell, then every 5 minutes I start selling, every 10 minutes, after that, every 30 minutes, every hour after that. I earn my average £60 a day, then sometimes I don't sell from the start, every 1 hour, 2 hours, 3 hours, I only sell 1 or 2 products but in the middle of the day I start selling and at the end of the day, I sell increasingly, until I sell 12 merchandise, then I reach an average of £60 a day. So sales come at different times, so you have to work the full 8 hours because you don't know what time a customer will come to buy your everyday goods or services.

It's Not Easy to Make £300 a Week

When it comes to running a business or selling products or services, I won't lie to you, that it's easy. You have to work hard to make money because some people will tell you that they love your product or service, but they end up giving you excuses to say no to buying your product. Yes, you have to do your work to get your product out to numerous people. Customers giving you money for your goods is not charity, if you don't work, you don't eat, you have to work hard for your money.

Have a Motivation

When you enter a life of selling products, a life where you work to satisfy the needs of customers, their wants, you have to ask yourself what do I get out of this, that is after you sell the products you make and when everyone is as happy as you want them to be, to be awarded or rewarded to make you happy? For example, if you earn £1000,000, what do you want? Many people want a luxury house with many bedrooms in the most prestigious areas where the rich people live, some want to drive sports cars, do you want a Ferrari, Porsche, Driving Phantom Rolls-Royce, Land-Rover? Do you want a Lamborghini? And some desire to take care of mum and dad, take them on holiday, make sure they are happy, some wishes to help the poor, what Do you want too? Some people do it for their girlfriend, they want a great marriage, some people want to educate their children in rich schools like Eton School, King's College, Cambridge to become politicians, etc So you have to have motivation, something that encourages you, and if you succeed in conquering, you can also be happy, you can not only make the world happy with your product or service, and you will not get anything, really not, you have to pay yourself.

Differences in Customer Experience

Many customers would like to experience the customer experience, to taste the product before they buy it. Some people would like to experience what your product is and how it feels, how it works, how fun it is, or the benefits of the product, but that doesn't mean they want to buy, so customers are different.

Make a Pitch

If you're selling a product, don't sell a product and say, "This is my product, give me money, no!" First, prepare a story that fits your product or service because people love stories because I sell CDs from the top of town to the other end of town, people they tell me that they like my story, find out why I start with a greeting, then I smile I assure them that I am a friendly person, come calmly, so they are comfortable to receive me for a conversation, and for a mirror effect, they smile at me because they trust me. I start introducing myself by saying my name. I tell them the offer or my story which is: I've made a music single, and I'm selling it for £5 if they're interested then it's up to them if they want to buy my product, but I've already told them my story, my name, the price of the item, if they are interested, they decide to buy they give me the money, and we follow steps to close the deal. So, you give a presentation and if you do it to 500 people, you sell 1 to 3, and if you do it to 500 other people, you sell 6, and if you do it to 1000 people, you sell 3, and so on until you have done the whole world, you become a rich man and if you use that system to sell online, and you create a website, go to google, Facebook, YouTube, imagine you make another £300 more weekly, then you increase it to £600, so that's multiplication. You also need to think about expansion, starting small.

Have Fun Selling Your Product

You know, selling is the most exciting thing! When I sell my CD every day, I smile and have fun with the customers. I love it, especially when I break through my average daily sales of £60+. I'm gaining a lot of confidence in it, it's starting to feel so good, and it's starting to be fun. I'm starting to enjoy talking to customers to the fullest, I'm not even looking at the money or stock any more. I start to get very excited about how customers react, and some customers refuse to buy my product and say they don't have cash, sorry, or they leave, or it's OK thanks but no, thanks. Some will even say that they know I want money, but they don't want to give it to me, so it all starts to look ridiculous to me, it's just fun, it's worth it selling your product to direct and indirect customers because even if they refuse to buy your products, you're still selling to enough people that it's purely fun and if you smile and enjoy interacting with customers, it's good for you, and laughter is good for your health and makes you live longer.

Stupidity Is Costly

Selling a product is a system. You have to work with a system that works with time, like husband and wife, a man can't have children without a wife, so both need each other to have children, so you have to work with the system and time, and at the end of the day, you will receive your sales results. The reason so many people give up on selling a product is because they don't know how to sell the product they are selling. So, it is important to have sales knowledge because knowledge is vital and stupidity is expensive.

Discipline & Consistency

The days of the sales are different, some days the product sales go fast, you make a lot of money, on average £60 a day, and some days the sales slow down, the product sells this hour, and it doesn't even sell after 3 hours, but at the end of the day, you get your average daily sales on a non-selling day like another best day. And this is a test to see if you are disciplined because you have to maintain discipline and consistency when selling, you should work with a system and time. If you know these two things, you will never be disappointed. If you know these two things, working with the system and 8 hours a day, you will never be disappointed in your sales activities, you will always achieve average sales and no one can stop you, if once you know how your business works, what the system is, when you know how much time it takes to talk to enough customers in a given day, i.e. 8 hours, and you know the average sales, how much money you make per day, week, month, year then you have to go through that process again and again like a circle, then you will prosper you will be successful. You will be a millionaire, billionaire, trillionaire, but people fail because if sales don't come early or come later than they expected, they get frustrated and say ah it doesn't work so always work with the system and the system on the right, and time on the left, you will succeed with the product or service you are selling.'

How Thinking of Budget Affects Sales

Selling directly to the customer, coming up with a budget and putting it in your head like rent, transport money and other bills is not good because you forget the good attitude you need to sell your product to the customer, you forget to smile, you forget to get excited, you forget attitude, and you start talking to customers like a robot and the more you do that, the more you don't connect and interact with customers, when a customer says no, it starts to influence and hurt your attitude, and before you know it, you start focusing more on the sale, and when the sale doesn't happen, you start telling yourself:

it doesn't work, there's something wrong with my product, or you start to say people don't love your product. Don't think about budget and keep a good attitude in working hours and focus on using the system and going with the numbers. Remember, sales are just a numbers game, so go through the numbers and get your average £300, weekly income and standard criteria for creating a small business.

Attitude

When it comes to sales, your attitude is your most important asset. What is an attitude? My sales experience shows that attitude is a smile on your face. Attitude is your enthusiasm the tone of your voice, the way you speak, your body language your politeness when approaching the customer (for example, this is my attitude and my attitude towards the customer hello I'm Mathias I have a musical single I'm selling it to everyone for £5.00, are you interested?) that's the attitude I'm showing. I'm impressed with this product. I am very excited to seeing you (the customer) today, and I am very excited to tell you about this product that I have, and you will benefit greatly from it. I'm selling it for £5 so that's

23

my attitude, that's how I win, so my attitude is very essential. Protect your attitude when selling and when you are faced with various noes, some customers will be rude, some will smile and say no, and others will want to give you money but change their minds in the process, so what you need to do is protect your attitude, when you hear no, or when you hear clients making excuses, just move on to the next client because the more noes you get, the closer you are to yes, and with that honest, sweet, interesting attitude to the next client, your day will be good, and you will reach your average sales goal!

Sales Are Just a Game`

Making £300 a week means talking to enough people about your product or selling products by getting enough people to buy from you. Because you can't expect to talk to 10 people and get sales for your product, you need to go over an infinite line of people talking to them, pitching your product to them to get £300 from that endless line over and over again. Get £300 this week by talking to 14,000 people and next week get £300 by talking to another 14,000 people, and you get another £300 by talking to another £14,000, but you can't talk to 10 people and expect to get £1,200 sterling per month, so it is not impossible to sale just using the system I am teaching you it is a proven system, it works, it is a business rule called the law of averages, it has existed in previous generations and is being used in the current generation by all businesses and will continue in the generations to come, you must understand that there is no stopping here, it's a one-way system That's how it should be. So, you have to understand how sales works, it's about numbers, it's about getting your product to the masses and from those masses of people that you speak to, your customers, your soldiers, the people who love your product, they will buy it and make you rich.

A Record of My Production

Now I have calculated my production which is £80 today, but I'm averaging £60 a day and when I calculated my production it was great. It's sweet, I'm satisfied, It gives me the energy to go back to work tomorrow. That way you earn £300 a week using the system and putting time into it, and you get your average turnover.

Marketing

Marketing is a way of selling a product or service. Marketing is the superstar, without marketing you are just lying to yourself. As a seller of a product or service, Eye and every year needs to see and hear your products offer and engage with you until they become loyal soldiers, loyal customers for life.

Discipline Is Very Important

Discipline is crucial the greatest man, Mike Tyson, said that "discipline is doing what you hate as if you love it." Today my product didn't sell for 30 minutes, then I took a break and saw that some government officials were grilling in Parliament Square, so I went to eat chips, hot dogs, salad, with those members of parliament, ministers, and excellent people of the country. At that place was a barbecue outside; thus I sat with them at one of their tables and they thought I was one of them, but I actually went there uninvited, and so they introduced themselves to me and one of them asked me who I was, but I would rather not say my name because I wasn't allowed to be in their club. It's for the civil servants and I just forced myself there, and I had a great time, I had a good time. I was excited to be with the lords of the land, so then I went to sell, and the sales happened quickly, one in 10 minutes, another in 20 minutes, another in 5 minutes, all went towards my production of £60 for the day. Until I worked a lot of sales because I had the discipline to not count my money until the end of the day because if I count it before I become lazy when I make enough money, or I can get discouraged if I make less, or it may make me think too much so at the end of the day, I knew I made money, I had a lot of money in my pocket because I sold a lot, so I was tempted to go home and stop working before the finish time, but I remembered the principles of working with the system and the schedule, which means I have to stick to my working hours, so I continued, instead of going home, So I made over £60 a day, so I rounded up the hours and made more sales which brought me an extra £20 which is a total of £80 so being disciplined and working 8 hours is very, significant

Success Tips for Selling

Success is about addition and multiplication, let's say you make an average £300 in sales per week. The next month you double that income to £600 a week, the next 2 months you triple it to £900, and after another 3 months you increase your income to £1200 a week by selling more products than you sold. Last month you keep multiplying by the last number then you are lucky, so add and multiply by the last number whatever you are selling. This is called success!

Who wants to be successful? Take your product and talk to 14,000 people a week, pitch them your product and sell it, do it for a whole year and see the result because the result you get from talking to 14,000 people, 70–80 people will like your product and because they like your product, they will refer you to other people, and before you know it, more customers like your product and people who like your product are buying every time you make it. Every time you sell it, those sales are enough to make you a lot of money. That's how you succeed as an entrepreneur, but you don't wait for success, it's not like that you have to act for action speaks louder than words!

Starting a Business From £300 a Week

So, when you can consistently make £300 a week over a period of 1 year, you need to start building a team of people to sell the same product for you so that you can multiply £300 a week to £600 a week and over a period of 3 calendar months from £60 a day to £120 a day to £10,000 a day over time, and you'll add more people to your team. You teach them how to sell products or services like you, you teach them how to make £60 a day, you teach them how to make £300 a week and when you teach 10, they bring you £300 a week each, then you become a company, and if you get them to train 10 more people, then you start expanding as president of that organization until you can appoint regional directors and owners for various offices or branches around the country to sell your product or service and earn millions.

Approaching Customers

When selling a product, it is important to be careful how you deal with the customer because the purpose of the sales conversation is to connect and build a relationship. Once this is established, the customers can trust you and decide whether to buy your product or not. Some people buy my product not because it's good, but because of how I treat them. They say I am very polite and friendly. Some say they like my charisma, others say I'm witty.

Chapter 3

3 Reasons Why Customers Buy

―――――――――※―――――――――

There are three reasons why a customer buys from you. Foremost, he/she is interested in the product or service you are selling, a customer has a desire, likes or is emotionally moved to buy your product or service. Secondly the ability to pay, customers must have the money to pay for the price you offer for the product. Therefore, broke customers can't buy even if they want your product because they don't have enough money. Thirdly is the payment method, you have to provide all the payment systems to take the customer's money, such as, card, PayPal, cryptocurrency, because some people still pay in cash these days and some people don't pay by cash, they only use cards or contactless. So if you're selling something and can only accept cash, you're going to lose customers because some card-carrying customers won't be able to buy what you're selling, even if they want to and even if they have the money to pay for it. So, as a seller and as someone who wants to build a business, you need to make sure that you have all the payment methods available for the customer to buy. Contactless or card payments require a card vending machine. You also need to have PayPal, stripes and bank transfers for online transfers and with stripes and other payment methods, you can sell your product and successfully sell your services.

Picture of Me and One of My Customers

The Game Is About People

So, the lesson is to understand people and your customers. As a salesperson, people are the game, people are the area where you play football to win your sales. You have to understand every person you talk to, how they buy and how they refuse to buy because people are your game. To play well and win the game, you need to understand the three types of customers you meet every day. Which are green, amber, and red.

Campaigning for the Presidency

Sales work, but you can't say you're selling something without telling the world about your products. It's like campaigning for the presidency, so you have to tell the whole world about your product, you have to tell everyone in the world one by one about your product and the service you offer, and when you reach the whole world, imagine 1 million people buying your product. Automatically. Makes you a multimillionaire, it gives you everything, it gives you cars, houses, a good life. But sell, sell, sell, talk to everyone about your product or service without getting tired one day at a time, one person at a time. You will make it. The definition of selling is: the activity of making products and services available to everyone so that people can buy them.

Paradise And Hell

So, as a seller, your sales are not the same every day, sometimes you can sell less, and sometimes you can sell more, so on Monday you can make £60 Tuesday £70 Wednesday £60 Thursday £50 Friday £60 Saturday £40 but still hit your weekly sales criteria, which is £300. I have always hit the benchmark every week so as a seller you should know that not every day is the same, some days are heaven and some are hells on earth, it boils down to weekly, monthly average, annual sales, revenue as well as profit and growth of your business, so you have to understand that not every day is rosy, some days are tough, it could be weather conditions or economic changes like the COVID-19 pandemic, a national recession or the change of seasons, but as you continue to working the basics of selling you will see your business grow. As a seller, you have to know your game, if you know your game, if you know your numbers, you will always win, so know your game.

Confidence as a Salesman

So selling is all about confidence. To be a successful seller who can sell a product every day for an average of £60 a day to £300 a week, you need to believe in yourself and your product, and believe in the sales system. So, you have to trust the system to talk to as many people as possible every day, This is how you sell. If you don't believe in yourself, the system, and your product, then you can't sell because you're ambivalent and think, oh, it's either going to work or it may not. You won't know for sure, but if you are confident, you will start talking to

2,000 people a day. With your product, you will get your £60 a day and when you talk to, 14000 and get £300 on average a week, then you're a winner, and you always win because you trust the product and the system.

That's the main point. You gain, and you build confidence when you test the system, and when you get results, you then start to do it like second nature. It will be fun and interesting, it will be like a game, an interesting game, a joyful game, so you need to trust that your product will sell, and you will sell because selling is a system. It's about numbers, it's a numbers game, it's repetition when you talk to everyone and offer them your product at a price. That's how you can win.

Reaching Criteria Qualifies You to Stay in Business

If you can't meet the criteria of £60 a day and £300 a week, you can't become an entrepreneur. Better go and work for someone else who can pay you a minimum wage of £300 a week. The reason is that the business is about criteria, if you can't make £300 a week selling your product how do you expect to pay the bills like transport, food, rent etc? Because selling your product means putting all your time and energy into it, that means spending all day all week on your business, so you need to make enough sales to survive and also save money to expand your business further if you plan to open. For example, in an office or shop, you have to do all these things.

To make enough money on a certain day of the week, so you must meet the criteria; otherwise you are just wasting your time and energy for nothing because not everyone is born to be an entrepreneur, not everyone is born to be a leader, some people are born to be led. They are born followers. They are born workers so if you try to do business, and it doesn't work out, be honest with yourself and find a job that will be easy for you with less time and hustle.

Reaching Criteria Multiplies Your Business

When you can meet the criteria of £60 a day and £300 a week, it means you've learned and understood how the sales process works, you can train other people and build a team to help you grow your business and reach the world because that's all you can give, what you have, you can't give what you don't have, if you can't get 60 pounds a day, 300 pounds a week means you're failing, and you can't teach anything. Then once you meet the criteria of £300 a week you will need to build a team to train them in the sales process, so, they can make more money for your business and you earn commission.

From their sales as the business grows and you get richer and richer.

The Most Beautiful Thing

The most beautiful and exciting thing in selling is the moment of exchange, when you have visited so many people to offer your product, and they say no, no, no, but when you tell the right customers, and they say yes and give you money in exchange for your product or service that you are selling it is the most beautiful moment, the moment of magic, is a miracle. It's like ecstasy, it's a happy moment I can't describe. It is the best thing about selling, giving your product in exchange for money and the value of money will give you a good life that will make you live in a nice house, drive a nice car, be a rich man and own the world, which is the best thing about selling, I think the description I can give is (The death roll) that time, the crocodile shows off its victory when it captures its prey by dragging it into the water. He rolls around in the water in the middle of the lake to celebrate and show that I have my prey. That's why I like to sell. It's the coolest thing I've ever done, I'll sell my way to a billionaire because it's cute. It's party time when a sale happens. Therefore selling makes you rich, So make money to the height of the mountain that no climber can reach.

Sales Are Nothing but a Speech

Selling is nothing more than talking about your product all day to as many people as possible, they may be two thousand, and out of the many people you give your speech to, 12 in one day will say yes and give you money, and buy your product and If you give your speech in a week to 14,000 and 72 claps for you and buy your product or service, in 5–10 years you will be a rich man. Or woman, why? Because every day, every week, every month, every year you give your speech and many people give you money that will make you richer. As I write this chapter of this book, I am in London bridge selling to my customers talking all day to customers about my product until I talk to 2000 people a day but among all those people a percentage will listen and fall in love with my product and give me money and gradually every week, every month, every year I get richer and richer because I know how to deliver my speech in such a way that people can communicate, connect and fall in love with my product, that is sales. Therefore, you should be happy to talk to everyone every time every day and give them your speech with joy and enthusiasm, look smart and look like a million dollars, a million pounds for elegant suits are business suits.

Crown of A Number One Rich Person

So, as a salesperson, my job is to casually talk to people, women, men, and offer them my product or service at the price I set on any given day. I speak to 2000 people and earn £60 a day at the end of the week. On average, I sell £300. No need to exaggerate, it's as simple as ABC, selling is simple. Your job is to talk to people every day. Speak to people, offer them your product with a story with a price and let them decide to say yes or no and earn money. Talk to 14,000 people in a week 48,000 people in a month offer them your product or service, and you will really make money, so it's not hard to make money. It's easy to sell a product it's hard when you don't know how to sell or if you don't know the sales game if you don't know how to play it then, it will be difficult for you to sell any product or service, but if you know that sales is a game of numbers, this game will be so easy for you because you know that you just have to read the numbers, you have to talk to the whole world, talk to them about the proposition that you are offering, you have to talk to them, one on one, as a group, on TV, radio, internet, billboards any way you can and eventually, you will win and get the rich man crown.

Chapter 4

Business School

Sales is not something you can just wake up and start doing all of a sudden. And become a millionaire in a day no learning how to sell is a process, a process, which starts with you understanding what it means to sell or trade I learned how to sell professionally when I was 30 years old, before that, I used to sell shoes and if I sold 1 or 2 shoes I would give up and say ugh that's not much money let me go do something else, but when I was 30 years old.

I went to a business program in London, Waterloo, called source marketing direct, and the regional manager was called Hector Montalvo, an American, the owner of the office I worked in, and they taught us how to sell. In that programme, we sold charity subscriptions such as British Red Cross, Cancer Research, British Heart Foundation etc. They taught us business rules, how to approach customers, how to handle a presentation, so first we learned sales theory, and then they made us to practice our pitch in the office before they sent us to the field or events in different parts of London (high streets or voltage stations) to sell to real people for 8 hours a day. It was a 9-month program and I first had to pass a test, consistently meet the criteria of £300 a week as a distributor and then to be promoted to leadership earning £350 a week consistently, which would qualify me to train other distributors to sell and earn £300 a week then own a branch or office, everyone had to build a team.

A leader and his distributors combined, they consistently had to earn £2,500 a week for two weeks in a row and if you did this for two weeks in a row they would will give you an office or branch and make you the manager of that establishment. To be able to grow and build your empire with a team of distributors that you trained to be just like you, but still have to belong to the organization or affiliate that you were in before you finished the training program, that was a fine plan. It was a good opportunity, but I failed I couldn't make £300 a week, I was unable to make £60 a day, I was unable to make £50. It's only on the road trips that I always reached the criteria of 60 a day.

And 300 a week and doing well more than everyone in the office until they crowned me king of the road trip because I always did more than everyone and became number one, but whenever I came back to London I made £15 a day and my highest earning in London was £25 a day and the program was superb many people apply in their thousands every year to join the scheme, but only 1% manage to take ownership and get offices to monitor and manage on behalf of the organization and what the office also does in terms of sales and profits. You still owe a certain percentage of commission to the previous owner or boss and the organization, which means you will continue to work for the organization.

Hector Montalvo Promised me A Land in Zimbabwe

Source Marketing Direct, Regional Director: Hector Montalvo

When I was doing so well on the road trips meant coming from London to start selling in places like Essex, Doncaster or Manchester just a different environment to sell to new people. It was like going to scout camp, so I got superb on the road trips to the point where I was doing better than the people on   the program before me and better than the people in London, so I got the manager's attention and the owner of our office, the regional manager, gave me a tour of the whole office and introduced me to some organization owners. He was very proud of me, and he said this guy has a talent for selling. Can you imagine, he has done better than everyone else in the office? When he goes on the road trips, he's number one, and the owner of the office, Hector Montalvo, the owner of the office promised me if I can consistently meet my criteria of £350 a week. And if I build a team of distributors and I meet the criteria of £2500 a week for two weeks in a row and they give me an office. He will come back with me to my country, Zimbabwe, and he will buy me land as a gift to build a house for me and my mother to live in. It was good for me because he was impressed and amazed by my talent to sell, but unfortunately, we all know the story when I failed, and I didn't get to have the land as my gift in the end.

The Objective of the Business Enterprise

The rationale behind the failure of 99% of individuals, including myself, who pursued the business program field, was due to our unsuitability for the position. We did not utilize the valuable information provided by the business enterprise to attain success and make £2500 per week within two weeks. However, the remaining one percent who implemented and applied the information to sell charities successfully, earned £300 per week and eventually generated £2500 within two weeks. They went on to establish offices and now earn approximately 15 grand weekly while enjoying their success. Having gained ten years of sales experience, I am now sharing my knowledge with the world. Those who take this information and apply it correctly will be the right individuals to advance their entrepreneurship and careers.

Closing a Sale

Finalizing a sale involves persuading the customer that your merchandise is the ideal solution for their needs, and that it will provide them with contentment. Closing the sale entails inducing the customer to accept your proposal, and when they do, they act on it by giving you their money and receiving your product. When you successfully close a sale, the customer stops contemplating and automatically hands over their money. Later, they realize that they have spent their money and cannot return the product, making it too late to seek a refund.

My vow to make millions

Therefore, the rule was that anyone who performed well for the week and beat everyone in the office to earn the highest money, £350+ weekly criteria would have to teach everyone the secret that made him triumphant, he was supposed to teach what worked for him, so that morning it was my turn and I taught everyone what worked for me. During my teaching back, I made a vow and told everyone: to achieve success is what I vow to live for and which I am ready to die for, no matter how long it takes. It was my promise that I would make millions in the future, no matter what. And everybody was very moved, and they all clapped for me and congratulated me.

My shameful exit out of business school

We started our day at 7:30 am, the office manager would come and open the door with the office owner, all the leaders will enter the building, go to the conference room? Before the distributors arrive at 8am, we would have meetings with the managers to discuss and plan the day. The events we would be going to assess our distributor's performance and growth, and we would coach them on areas, they needed to improve, the manager and owner would influence us with some training to teach the distributors on how to grow up and become like us. Distributors would come. We would train them in whatever area we thought they needed help with so they can sell to meet the criteria of

£300 every week and £60 a day, then one day we were in a meeting with the distributors and the managers and owners. And a distributor asked a question? Saying why is Mathias a leader, we don't see him ringing the bell (which was a culture in the programme. Whenever someone meets the criteria of £50 or £60 a day, they have to ring a bell in front of everyone as a celebration or announcement of their success) he doesn't meet the criteria every week. We've never seen him make £60 a day. Likewise, we haven't seen him make it in London, why is he a leader? Furthermore, we saw other leaders ringing the bell and reaching £60 a day. I was very embarrassed in front of everyone because it was obvious that I had failed the programme, and they we're not going to keep me there for long. After that meeting, the owner told me to stay behind, we needed to talk. Then the owner, Hector, said to me, Mathias, do you think this is for you? Do you think this business will work for you, and I answered yes it would, but in other words, he was informing me that I needed to quit and go home, so he let me go out to the field with everyone that day to do my work, but after another two weeks he asked me again Mathias, don't you think you should go and start doing something better with your life, you know you can save time and go find something which can give you more money instead of trying to do this business that won't help you, so I said OK, hector, I heard you? After that day, I never went back to that business programme because of the shame of failure. I accepted my fate, so I failed the programme.

I failed to buy my Fiancée her Audi dream car

When I entered the corporate program, I had high expectations, especially when I did well in road trips and when I was crowned king of road trips in the office for my high performance in making money and meeting the criteria. I then I told my Fiancée and asked what she would like me to buy for her if I had my own office and made a lot of money, and she said she wanted an Audi car and I promised to buy her a car and a good life, and she believed and was over the moon, but when I started failing the program, and she saw that I earn £100 a week in London. I felt bad, knowing I had disappointed her.

Furthermore, I had promised her a great life, a good life, that I would be a rich man, but everything fell apart, and I failed with gloom colors.

A decade after the Business School

And even though I failed the program, I am still working to fulfill my vow, so I keep going.It's now 10 years after leaving the programme, I'm still selling until I fulfill my dream to be rich. But countless people when they fail the programme, they are defeated and become a customer instead of a vendor, they start working as employees in companies, they're at the end of the road, so sometimes it's not okay to give up, If you know you have what it takes to survive, if you still see results, why not fight to live another day?

Pays for My Living

The product I sell pays for my living. I earn £60 a day, £300 a week selling 12 products every day at £5.00 each. With this money, I pay for rent, transport, food, clothes etc, and I am saving money as capital to start a bigger company which will give me millions from the knowledge I learned selling this product (CD) in London, UK.

I Have Made Thousands Selling My Product

I made thousands selling my product for £5 to many people all over town, communities. With this skill of selling, when you know how to fish, you are not given fish to eat every day, you fish your fish. So sales, it's a skill worth getting. Even if you start selling something from £1, you know how to sell something that costs £5, you know how to sell a product or service worth hundreds of pounds, even £600, before you know it, you're making money to take care of yourself and your family. Money which can buy houses, money to buy cars, money to buy the world and live well for yourself, why? Since sales is a skill that makes you rich, when you know how to sell, it's only a matter of time before you have a lot of money and become a millionaire and billionaire because you know how to sell, you have found your way to heaven.

You Are in Control

As a salesman, you control your life, you control your destiny, you fight every day to live another day, fight to win because if you don't win, if you don't sell your products, you will become poor and homeless like all the other defeated homeless people In life. Therefore, as a seller, you have to fight to sell your product or service, to people in society, it's a battle you have to win, and you win by playing well by selling more products than last week and selling a constant amount of your products every day if you sell 12 products per day, if it is 72 products per week, it must increase every week to ensure a growing income, and you can use the money as you like, take care of yourself, your family, cousins and relatives and other poor people, and generously support the charities of your choice with your donations, so now you know it's survival, war, a game. So be encouraged.

An Exciting Thrilling Happy Game

Selling to me is nothing but a fun and exciting game. I like to sell, I like to sell because when you sell, you can talk to anybody and get to know people's character. You can go to beautiful places and talk to beautiful people, great and small, whites, blacks, Chinese, Asians and you can talk to them about your product and it's exciting. I sell my product for £5 a day and at the end of the week, I make an average of £300. I feel good. I sell my product in the city. Sometimes in the summer in the park near Buckingham Palace, Clapham Common and at the same time it's fun and social, it's healing and healthy for a person, and when I take breaks from sales, I eat great food, go to nice restaurants, talk to people everywhere, so I have customers everywhere because I sell my products directly, I go to communities, I sell my products in bars, pubs, shops, cafés and on the street because now as I write this book I am in Soho West End, UK capital, UK and I sell my products to all people in and outside the city, I love to sell, I love selling is nothing but a game and if you know how to play, you will always win, and that makes me rich. Likewise, I am happy the more products I sell, the more I earn, the richer I will be, wow!!

Picture of One of My Customers

Chapter 5

Sales to a Customer Are Automatic

Sales are automatic, as a seller, your job is just to go through the numbers and from the many numbers you go through offering and selling your products to people, you get a percentage of the customers who will give you your average income, every day of the week, monthly and yearly for the product you sell, so if you know sales is automatic or a system that works and repeats itself over and over again you can sell any product or service in hundreds, thousands, millions, and billions, therefore, offer the product to everyone and out of many people you offer to a certain percentage, will say yes and give you money and make you rich, you will create a successful business, so sales are automatic. A system which repeats itself so as a salesman or saleswoman just take your product, have your pitch or your story and go through the numbers, and you will have your wins you will have your gains you will have your buyers, so sales are automatic like an automatic car, your job is to just drive it and know the buttons to press.

And know the destination you are going to (vision).

In Africa There Is a Saying

Which says a baby who doesn't cry on his/her mum's back dies. Which means a baby should cry to mum as a signal to communicate his/her needs, whether it's a feeding or a diaper change, so you can pop the question? Where can I get customers to buy the product I have, or where can I start? Distributing them, or how can I sell my services, you may ask? It's simple, the first thing you have to do is open your mouth and tell the whole world that you have a product or service, and you're selling it for this amount and if people get this product, they'll like it, they'll experience it, and they'll benefit, so first talk to your family, your neighbors, your community, your city, your country and all the countries of the world, then you will achieve your business goal of being the richest man or woman in the world with more money than everyone.

Who Is the Greatest Salesman or Saleswoman?

He/she is the one who successfully distributes his product to all 8,000,000,000 people living in this world today.

Definition of Vision

Vision is visualizing or imagining how much your business can grow. You need to set goals and achieve them to reach the height you envision your business to grow. Let's say "I'm starting to sell doughnuts" if I see myself selling doughnuts to 10 people in my neighborhood, in my lane where I live, and if I see that in 5 years we're expanding and selling nationwide, and in 15 years selling to billions of people around the world, that's a vision, but some people have no vision, they just go with the flow, it doesn't matter if they sell one doughnut today and two doughnuts tomorrow, they will be happy, and if they sell 10 doughnuts next week, they are happy and satisfied, they don't take time to think and imagine, How their business can become great, and they don't take the time to explore the full potential of their business to set goals that need to be met to grow the business, to paramount potential.

Why Is It a Game

Selling is a game for me because I know exactly how many products I will sell per day, week, month and year. I know exactly how many people I intend to sell my products to, and I know how to pitch that product to them. I know how they would react negatively and positively before they buy, and I also know how to ask them for money and give them their product in return, so that everyone is happy. I love to sell, even in my dream I can sell millions and billions of products because I learned to sell 12 products a day, I gained the knowledge and experience to sell 72 products a week. I learned to sell for 1200 pounds a month. The product is priced at £5.00, making the sale the equivalent of eating the best African food or McDonald's. I'm a winner when it comes to sales. I can sell anything, I can sell real estate, I can sell cars, I can sell a pen, I can sell anything.

Psychology

Selling is Psychology. Selling is nothing more than a mind game or mind reading because playing this game psychologically means knowing the mind of the customer and how they think and feel during the sales process. The first step is to offer the product in a way that your customer will perceive as valuable and useful, and in a way that they feel they need or want it, or the way you attractively create the presentation. Second, you need to know what the client will say to reject your offer, and the negatives they will give you reasons to say no. You need to know how to handle and overturn those negative objections. You have to know how to repurpose your product to convince them. You also must know how to ask for money, so when you know what your customer is thinking, when you know what they want, you win. So explore your customer's mind, know what they want, handle their objections!

Ingredients Of Selling Successfully

Hard work and smart thinking are the ingredients of success. If you don't have a smart brain when you work hard, forget about success because you are not using the ingredients that create success. For example, the famous British chef Gordon Ramsay or Jamie Oliver have numerous restaurants across London.

How can they make the most delicious delicacies without the necessary Ingredients? Or how can I, being from Zimbabwe, prepare my main dish sadza ne Nyama: without cultural ingredients? It wouldn't taste good, would it? It won't work, so I have to get the ingredients to make the most delicious dinner. Hard work and intelligence are the ingredients of success.

Coca-Cola Is the Best Selling-Drink

An example of a good salesperson is Coca-Cola. This company knows how to sell its drink Coca-Cola, which is the most sold drink in the world every day. Everyone drinks Coca-Cola at home, in shopping streets, restaurants, department stores, bars, schools, offices, government offices, even the palaces of the king and Queen, the White House, so you must learn from Coca-Cola. There is a saying in the Bible that says who can succeed the king, but the one who does what the king has already done, so to be successful you have to learn from success Coca-Cola has led the way in making money, and now you have knowledge, and knowledge is power. Allow this knowledge to make you start from nothing to the maximum riches.

Advertisement

The success of selling a product is directly and indirectly talking to many people about the product through every available avenue, online advertising, media and direct conversation with people in the field.

Selling Higher Tickets

So now I have learned how to sell 12 products a day at £5.00, now how about when I start selling a £100 product. If I sell a product for £100 in one day, I will earn £1200. A day. I use the same system and I will talk to the same number of people, I am reaching now so out of the 2000 people I talk to I make £60 because I price my product at £5.00 and if I have a product. I sell £1000 to those 2000 people a day that alone means I make £12,000 a day and if I start selling cars for £20,000 that means I make £240,000 a day and if I start selling houses for £1,000,000 pounds sterling and I will approach the same number of people in a day, and that means I will make £12,000,000 a day selling just 12 homes using the same system I learned to sell 12 products a day at £5.00 each.

Distribution

If you don't have the spirit of distribution to distribute your product to your neighbors in your community to your country to all countries, you can't have much success, so distribution is important. Therefore, distribute your product to your target market to all customers who want to buy your product (lovers of your products) if you want your product to reach soccer players, you need to make sure you distribute your product to all soccer stadiums, soccer clubs and soccer countries and everything related to football.

Smart Wear

It's important to look like a million bucks in smart wear. It means a lot to the client, builds confidence, is professional, confirms the seriousness of the business and makes people take you seriously.

Daily Routine or Formality

So today I was out (where the customers are) and I went to this coffee shop called (knows) and I wanted to contact their customers to introduce them to my product. The lady working there came and said sir you can't keep coming here to talk to our customers and I said no they are for all of us, so customers are for anyone as long as you offer a product or service to any customer. This world is for you and every company that offers products to them, but you have your percentage, other companies have their percentage, everyone has a market share, it's a share game and customers are provided for everyone.

Hard Work Kills

I have awful body aches that I have to relieve by resting, like sleeping and sitting comfortably. Why? I work hard every day selling up to 8 hours from pub to pub, restaurant to earn £300 a week, which is a weekly benchmark I meet every week. Now I need to create other streams of income so that I don't go under due to this pain. I need to add indirect marketing and start selling my music products online because it will increase my income or the hard work will kill me. So, the lesson is that hard work without smart thinking kills, that's why some people quit their jobs. Because of health problems like back pain, bad arm, bad leg, bad vision, etc. because they do the same thing for so long without planning to scale and grow, that's why the saying goes don't put all your eggs in one basket because if something happens, they all fail, and you lose everything, so that means you are not dependent on one income but create many more channels they will bring you high income and will ensure you have more than enough.

Have the Mind of an Owner

Every business has a manager, an owner and staff, and a business is an idea that you have to offer a service or product to people for money, so if you can make £300 a week and £1200 a month, you should start by thinking about upskilling and shifting responsibility up the hierarchy, down to grow your business because as long as you do everything yourself, your business will stay small because you are only one person, and you can only do so much and your time is limited, and the whole world is waiting for your goods. So as a business owner, your job will be to work hard thinking to scale and grow the business, but not doing the physical day-to-day sales work, but thinking micro and teaching your staff how to create a product, manufacture, distribute and sell. to customers, In other words, you are the brains of your business, so think about it.

As a Salesperson, Customer's Attention Is Your Money

When customers can give you their attention, know that you will earn because they will listen, consider and decide. Most people will say no, but a good enough percentage of people will say yes and give you money, so it's your job as a seller to look for attention, searching for people who can pay attention to you and can engage and connect with you, for example, I was at London Bridge and three people were sitting at a table in a café, 2 men and a woman were enjoying their food, eating, drinking and talking, so I went to their table and when I started talking to them and selling my products in front of the two of them, a man and a woman paid attention to me and when I told them about me and said, "my music is for this amount if you are interested" and they said okay, maybe next time but after that when I walked away from the table, one of them, who ignored me when I was talking to the two, said: Have you noticed that I did not participate? Because I know that if I participate and engage with the seller more often I will begin to desire his product and I will say yes and buy it, and everyone started to laugh. So, I can guarantee you that one of those people bought my product at some point after that meeting because I kept visiting them, getting their attention, and I kept connecting and pushing my products to them. That's why attention is key, both online and on TV or Radio attention is your money. As a salesperson, you work with people's attention because if they pay attention to you, there is an opportunity to sell.

The Greatest Mathematician Is a Salesperson

Because he knows how to calculate his way to becoming a millionaire and how to turn that calculation into a reality by selling his product, There is the wealthy owner of the Chelsea football club, Abramovich, ordinarily I'm in town, I always drop by his Chelsea football club. But this man Abramovich started selling plastic dolls in the market, then he started selling oil and became so rich that now he owns a football club. The salesman knows how to count, he knows how to reach a million pounds, he knows how to reach 100,000,000 pounds, he knows how to reach a billion, selling a simple product at a basic price to people. Like Elon Musk, Amazon owner Jeff Bozos, Apple computer founder Steve Jobs, Microsoft founder Bill Gates and Mark Zuckerberg, Facebook, Richard Branson, Virgin Airlines are brilliant and skilled at sales. In the game. They know the numbers. They know how to calculate the known numbers 1+1=2, so they know that if they sell an item at £5, if they multiply £5 x 5 = £25, they know they can sell 5 products. Earn 25 pounds, and they understand how much people they have to speak to get that 25 pounds as income. They know they have to sell countless products to make a lot of money to get rich, so I really admire and congratulate these successful entrepreneurs of the world.

Sales Mathematician

Thus, I also became a mathematician, which means that now I have a vision: I will not be a musician to reach the level of Jay-Z, Michael Jackson or other celebrities, but I will go into business because I learned sales and have taught them in this book. I will use these basics. I will use this system and put it to work to make me a millionaire and a billionaire, how? Likewise, I have been working as a web designer for the past 6 years. I learned how to build websites and I started building websites for people and businesses 6 months ago.

But now I have a new client coming to me every week with £300 each and I have also started a kid's bookshop that sells children's books, so I'm starting these businesses and putting this system and fundamentals into practice so that it can make me a millionaire and a billionaire! I learned how to design websites and how to create websites for ordinary people and large companies. Therefore, when I calculate my income from web design, the average income is currently £1200 per month, so my math to become a millionaire is this: I will aim to sell 12 sites per week, which will bring me £3,600 x 4 = £14,400 per month, so £14,400 a month x 12, I can earn £172,800 a year, that's more money than the UK prime minister gets. Boris Johnson, the Prime Minister of the UK, earns £80,807 a year, but I will make £172,800 selling 12 sites a week at £300. How will I do This? In the system I described in this book for 12 sales a day, I talk to 2,000 people, which means I will talk to 2,000 regular people and business owners to get 12 willing people. The mission and goal is to do it in one week. Therefore, as I aim to sell 12 websites a month, which means I will talk to 48,000 people a month. Ordinary people, entrepreneurs needing a website. But I have to take baby steps, one step at a time. This is my mission and my plan so if I earn £172,800 a year, that means I'll be a millionaire in the next five years just from building websites in the next five years. You see, I think like a millionaire now because I know how to sell an item for £5. When I'm a millionaire I'll be a mathematician again and find a way to get £100,000,000.

When I have £100,000,000 I will find a way to join the billionaires club and then the job will be done, which is a system and math that anyone can apply to their business, regardless of what you sell.

My Book Has to Make Me a Million and Above in Sales and Profits

I need this book I have written to make a million pounds, furthermore, if I sell a million books I will be a millionaire, that's right, so now the mission is to sell 12 books a day for £11.99. Return £143.88 per day £1,007.16 per week How will I do this? Create a website and sell those books on my website, I will use social media and promote that book; I will sell that book on Amazon, I will distribute that book on eBay, I will distribute that book to many online bookshops, I will convert it into an e-book and audiobook and sell it, then I will distribute that book through all the popular distribution channels so that it makes money, so this book will bring in over a thousand a week, so that's the mission, that's the plan, I want this book to make me a millionaire in five years' This book will sell because I am the sales driver because I trust the sales system. I'm a firm believer in the numbers game, and this book will be sold even in supermarkets like TESCO and ASDA. If this book teaches people how to make millions and build a billionaire's business, it must also make me a millionaire. I know this book looks simple, But there are secrets in it to change someone's life from rags to riches, from living impoverished to becoming a millionaire because knowledge is power and information is precious, the knowledge in this book is life changing. That's why the knowledge in this book is life-changing, and that's why the knowledge I'm giving away is worth millions and billions. Therefore, this book should give me something useful it is good, I am happy with it. I am satisfied with it.

Chapter 6

I Have Come Across Many Famous People

So, I have sold and made these thousands of pounds, as I describe in this book. I've met numerous famous people. I met some members of the royal family, and I was part of the crowd when I saw the Duke and Duchess of Cambridge, William and Kate Middleton, As they left the Noel Coward Theatre, Leicester Square In St Martin's Court WC2 City of Westminster, I met David Javid, the first Asian to become Chancellor and who is now the UK's Health Secretary. I met him while I was selling he was in Parliament Square, Westminster, by the Treasury near Number 10 Downing Street, I have seen Prime Minister Boris Johnson and his motorcade on more than 4 occasions as they drive through town, and I have met Manchester City's forward, Raheem Sterling

who scores plenty of goals for Manchester City and England and earns £300,000 a week. He was coming out of a hotel in Carnaby Street at night and I said hello to Sterling, and he said hi big man and I asked if I could take a selfie, and he ignored me and got into a black van with his friends, and they took off in two black vans and I met a famous dancer on Oxford Street when he walked into JD with his girlfriend and people were asking him for autographs. I met many famous people! I met a Hollywood producer who made big budget movies, and he gave me money for my music,

On my right is Simon, the BBC newsreader In Front of The Groucho Club, Dean street W1 City of West-Minster in Soho.

I met the BBC news anchor Simon in a bar near the BBC studios, and met him again at the Groucho Club restaurant in Soho. I met Dermot O'Leary, the man who hosted the BBC's Big Brother. On Portland Street near the BBC studios, I met music producer John Harvey, who lives In England and South Africa, I met the famous comedian Paul Chowdhry, who works for the BBC and ITV.

On my right, Paul Chowdhry

He films documentaries and does stand-up comedy, he ate at the Soho restaurant opposite the Prince Edward Theatre on Old Compton Street and his bodyguard was there, and many people came up to him and taking

Picture of Me and Ryan

selfies with him, I met Ryan, one of the singers behind the famous soul song Just Imagine, which is always played on smooth radio, drinking with friends at the bar opposite Nando's in Soho, I met another man who became the number one idol and he and his girlfriend went for a drink in one of the bars along Regent Street and I met a famous actress who acted in Mission Impossible alongside Tom Cruise, a famous American actor, I met Idris Elba in Covent Garden. He got out

of the car and was surrounded by bodyguards. I waved at him, and he smiled and walked past on his way, I also met 3 close servants of Her Majesty Queen Elizabeth II,

On my right Prince Charles, Chief of staff

And I asked all of them? How it was like working with her Majesty Queen Elizabeth and they said it was nice. I met Prince Charles, chief of staff outside Clarence house on the wide road leading to the front of Buckingham palace. I met the Russian correspondent Steve Rosenberg in Carnaby Street in one of the famous bars.

On my left is Steve Rosenberg, Russia news Editor

So, I met government officials, renowned musicians and I met great People selling my simple music product. I also met Matthew Avery Modine an American actor who acted in a Steve Jobs film as a former

In the top picture on my right is Matthew Avery, Modine is an American actor and filmmaker, who rose to prominence through his role as U.S. Marine Private/Sergeant J.T. & Joker & Davis in Full Metal Jacket.

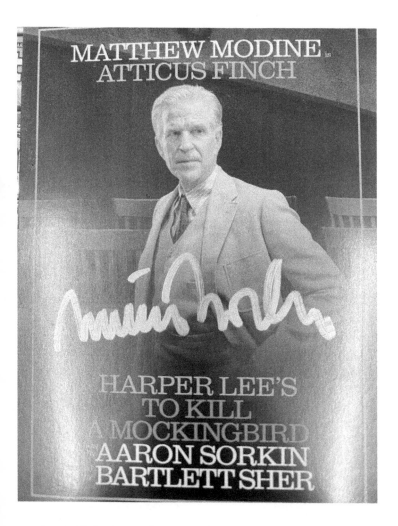

MATTHEW MODINE is
ATTICUS FINCH

HARPER LEE'S
TO KILL
A MOCKINGBIRD
AARON SORKIN
BARTLETT SHER

Pepsi CEO, I met him in Soho. He was signing autographs backstage of the Gielgud's theater, Rupert street W1, City of Westminster and I approached him and said I know you, you are that guy who acted in Steve Jobs' film, he smiled and said yes it's me, come see my show I am performing in the theater and he gave me the leaflet above. Lastly, I met Matt Smith in Whitehall, Great Scotland Yard Sw1 in a Pub called the Clarence. He was sitting down with his friends having a drink, I offered him my

Matt Smith on the right in the Crown Netflix film acting as the Duke of Edinburgh Prince Philip

product and he bought it through one of his friends using a contactless card because he had run out of cash in his wallet, so he asked one of his friends to make the payment instead. And I asked if I could take a selfie with him, but he said no, but he signed an autograph for me instead.

I am happy and excited about it. That's why I like selling because you never know who you're going to meet, especially in the city. People go there to have fun and relax, so I meet all kinds of people, both big and small. and not to forget, I also met Adedoyin Olayiwola "Ade" Adepitan MBE (born 27 March 1973) is a Nigerian-born British television presenter and wheelchair basketball player.

Picture of and Adedoyin Olayiwola "Ade" Adepitan in theNo2 Rose & Crown Pub in Mayfair he was hanging out with his colleagues.

As a presenter, he has hosted a range of travel documentaries and sports programmes for BBC television. Adepitan is a disability advocate and one of the first physically disabled television presenters in the UK, with a career of over 20 years.

Chapter 7

Selling Is a Process of Collecting Yes Decision

From customers all day long and one analogy I can give you is that sales is like picking ripe grapes in a vineyard, every day you go out in the field and look for ripe grapes to pick and enjoy the wine that is made from them, you don't bother with the noes because you know it's sour grapes, so you check up on them every time until they're ripe to be harvested. When I started selling in business school, I was so affected and crushed by the noes when I didn't make the sales, but now that I'm immune to noes, I realize that the noes are part of the sales, so you have to love them and be happy when a customer refuses to buy your product, knowing that one day they will buy it anyway, when they decide and when they are ready.

You Are controlling the Sales Conversation

As a salesperson, it's very, crucial to know that you can kindly interrupt people's conversations with and without their consent, and briefly get their attention with a brief introduction about yourself and offer them your product, and then they will decide yes or no to buy your product, then you can end the conversation with them and divert their attention away from you and let them continue their conversation.

Pricing

Allow people to pay a fair price for your product based on the market price. Don't charge too much and don't charge too little, but charge a price that is reasonable to support you and save enough to make the business reach its full potential because the purpose of selling is to drive the business to success. Grow and do more, stick to your set prices and hold the reins because if you are not strong, the customers will set the prices for you, but sporadically, you can make an exception.

The Best Way to Grow as a Salesman or Saleswoman

Take your product, get out there and go to people person to person—those people will encourage you, push you forward, make you a successful businessman or woman. Most people will say no to you, but those few who give you money are enough to make you rich. They will be your daily support and encouragement, and those who don't give you money will teach you as well how they want you to serve them. They will teach you how to create the perfect product that they want, so sales is a school. Every day you are in front of customers is a school you go to and get corrections and the day after that you come back and get a 10/10 passmark, so your teacher is your customers and your best business builders are your customers, and your customers will help you and encourage you.

Take your vision to the world and be successful, they say the customer is king. Without the customer a business is nothing, you are nothing but the customer is the king and Queen of everything you sell, so treat them and respect them because a customer is worth a thousand pounds, a million pounds and a a billion pounds because they put food on your table.

Your Way Out

So if you're selling, you're on your way out of poverty, you've got to sell your way out of the middle class, you've got to sell your way into millionaire and billionaire status because as a seller, you're controlling your destiny, it's in your hands to succeed or fail.

Expenses to Start the Breakdown

So, I would like to split the capital, costs, and profits from starting a business or selling a CD that has made me thousands of pounds. I buy a pack of 100 blank CDs every week. I burn the songs I made onto 72 blank CDs and sell them for £5 each and my total income would be £60 a day, £360 a week. So, the total cost is £10 per week, the profit is £350 per week. That £10 got me £360, therefore I'm making £350 a week, £1,440 a month in profit, and those 4 of my songs cost £150 a song to produce, so my starting capital was 4 songs x £150 = £600 + £10 for a pack of 100 blank CDs = £610 so that was my capital to start selling my music product and the profits I made in return.

Expecting to Get a Sale

So if you prioritize the distribution of the product before you expect to get the sale, that's the best way to generate sales to make money. Because if you prioritize sales and say you want to sell, you're saying I aim to make money. £300 a week as your number one priority, then you are just doing things for the money instead of satisfying the needs of the customer but the customer has to be the first to receive the product, you are selling and be happy that should be the priority, so the sale should automatically be something that happens naturally as you approach many numbers through the sales system to get an average percentage yes sales become automatic, let customers buy of course, but you focus on delivering the product to the customer you are more likely to succeed but if you just like the money, but you aren't concerned about the customer, you don't want the conversation, you don't want the customer to review, then you miss it.

Richer and Richer

Sales is a job where you swim in money. The more money you make, the more you spend with it and the more products you sell, the richer and richer you Become.

Good Luck

It takes a lot of luck to sell and be successful in business. Giving to the poor, the Bible says that those who give to the poor "lacks nothing" so if you always give to those who are less fortunate, such as churches, orphanages, the homeless, widows, charities, street beggars, and your poor relatives. Giving generously to the needy brings luck, happiness, and favor Because when the receiver says thanks for your generosity. That thanks turn to a blessing to you. Then what you give you get back many times or multiplied, for example, the top ten richest men in the world, like Bill Gates, Warren Buffett, Mark Zuckerberg, donate billions to charities and the more they give, the richer they become and are consistently in the top 10 billionaires club, so giving brings happiness.

Born With a Star

As for me, my star shines when I sell my products because it gives me satisfaction, joy and the best sense of achievement.

Picture of me and my music fans

I get so much attention from the customers I talk to, and it's lovely, and it means the world to me because this is where I see sales every week, month, year. It makes me rich, wealthy and a happier person, a happy person, so if you are a seller, or want to start a business, get up, go sell, and let your light shine bright, so that the whole world can see. What are you waiting for, let your star shine and if you sell thousands and millions of products, you will become rich and wealthy, and you will be satisfied and enjoy your reward.

What Selling Will Teach You

Sales teaches you how to make decisions to say yes or no to a purchase of a product, and also teaches how people make decisions about everything in every aspect of their lives, such as how they make decisions about marriage, having children, going to college, wearing certain clothes on a certain day, or general decisions in communication. Sales gives you the psychological knowledge of how people make yes or no decisions.

The Embarrassing Side of Being a Salesman

When you are selling during the day, when you get a lot of noes, until they knock you out emotionally and physically, and you ask, thinking, what's going on here, why aren't my product selling, and because of some customers being rude, if you are not strong, you can be so embarrassed that you can answer the customer and get mad at him or her and ruin your business, but as a seller if you play the game it's all just a process of reading the numbers and that at the end of the day, you get average sales, so you can take the heat and be able to endure rude customers who like to embarrass you, and you can smile at them. And thank those customers and wish them a good day and the customer will be satisfied that you will understand that it is fine if they ever refuse to buy your product, but that is the awkward side of the sale, as a seller, you have to be ready to take the fight and the heat, you have to withstand all the thousands and millions of noes to sell your products successfully. Because with many noes come yeses that will make you rich, so you have to be resilient you must sell, sell until you become a sales machine who doesn't care about "no" and shame from rude customers who look at you like an idiot, but you're not an idiot. You win sales for your work, so you have to be fierce like a lion and become the red lion of sales.

Preparation

One Sunday I went to a restaurant in Surrey and it was raining. People love this restaurant so much, and I love it myself, so I went there for dinner. But it was raining and other restaurants and pubs had tents outside because they couldn't seat many people inside, but only a few people could sit inside due to the COVID-19 restriction. So, I went there to a restaurant that I like, but there was no tent outside, and there was another customer in line in front of me. It was raining, and the waiter asked if I wanted to eat, and I said yes. Therefore, he asked me to sit in the rain, and he said can I clean your chair because it was wet and raining, so I said no, I can't sit in the rain? How can I enjoy my food in the rain, so the worker wanted me to sit outside where it would rain on me. Therefore, as you can see, the business owner was not prepared enough to have tents for the customers to sit outside in bad weather. I don't understand why he was careless, is it because he was too lazy to rent a tent or because he didn't have enough money, I don't know, but a businessman like the owner of this restaurant is a loser because if he doesn't, want to pay for the tents, and he expects the customers to still buy from him, then he is a loser, imagine how many days he lost customers because of the rain, but he would rather not invest in a tent. Where the customers can sit, and the customers will still pay for the tent when they buy food, and he, as a business owner, he can take some money from his earned profit and reinvest that money into his business to buy tents for customers, but he chooses not to, so he is a failure, and if he continues like this after 2–3 years, he will still lose money and go out of business, and he'll wonder what's going on, why people aren't buying, why his customers are dwindling, or why his business is failing because he didn't prepare for bad weather or any circumstances. It is essential to prepare your business if you know it will rain, rent tents and let customers sit in tents, but you cannot be careless to customers leaving them in the rain and still expect them to give you money. That's not how things work.

Hard Work Is a Talent

Not everyone can work hard. Some people can only work 8 hours a day, and they are tired. They go home, eat and sleep, but if you can work two or three times as much as everyone else, then you have talent. That talent will bring you success and reward you with riches and wealth, while the sleeper only has poverty. And the lazy weak link will be poorer and poorer and always begging, so if it's a talent, then selling is the best thing I ever had and never will have, because that talent has given me money and will make me richer, that's why I like to sell. I can sell 24 hours a day. I can talk to people 24 hours a day about my product and get people to say yes and give me their money to get rich. Because when you sell, you create a campaign for people to make you rich and get you into the clubhouse of millionaires and billionaires like Elon Musk, Bill Gates, Warren Buffett and Jeff Bezos. Just like people campaign for the presidency, salesmen, or women also campaign for the office of the 1st billionaire. If you are a salesperson selling anything, your goal should be to become the number one billionaire, not just sell without any direction.

Selling Makes One Powerful

Selling will make you a powerful man or woman, like the most powerful man on earth, Bill Gates, Françoise Bettencourt Meyers, Warren Buffett, Jeff Bezos, Richard Branson and Mark Zuckerberg, Elon Musk and many other rich people. Those rich men and women contribute a lot to the country's economy, they are responsible for the economy and the world. Politicians recognise them and benefit from their investment in their political parties; they are powerful, strong, celebrated and respected.

Mother and Father of Business

Sales grow your business, the more you sell, the more your business will grow and make billions and trillions, but if you don't make enough sales, there is no room for growth, you continue to struggle, and therefore selling is the foundation of business, marketing, and distribution is the mother of business a product or service does not sell itself. It's the driving force, it's the campaign you hold behind it. That's why as a seller, you have to talk to everyone face to face, directly and indirectly through your offers on the street, in their homes, on television, billboards and any kind of advertising, and when people see the product, they will begin to desire it, consider it, they will think about it and make a final decision and act to buy your product and make you rich. You also need to run an online campaign to market your product speaking to anyone online so that they visit your website, see your offer, click the buy button and pay with their credit card, giving you money, the product doesn't sell itself, but the salesperson is responsible for running the campaign and making a lot of noise and get people to vote with their wallets, then the job is done, the product now leaves your warehouse Into the hands of the people who are your customers.

The Praises My Customers Give Me

Here's what my clients tell me:

—You're funny

—You are a bistro

—You are a guru

— You are a star

—I like your driving

— You are a genius

—you are a professional

—you are one step ahead

— You know your game

— You're a hero.

—We love you man

—we are impressed

—I like your step

—I like your style

— You are smart

—You are modern

—You have mastered this game

—You are the red lion

—You are number one

—You know how to sell

—You are smooth, you are king, a master of game

—You are savvy

—You are a great salesman

—You are a Legend

and you have a lot of energy, that's why we love you, and I'm happy with these accolades because I also love my customers, they are also fun and have a lot of energy, that's why I love them. Our relationship is all business.

The Nos Come Like a Bullet

So, the noes come like a bullet, but you have to protect yourself in a bulletproof, like laughing at them when a customer tells you a hard no, dance a joyful dance, but be careful how you dance the noes out, go aside where the customer doesn't see you, then you can laugh and dance the noes out to bring yourself up or to encourage yourself to keep a happy attitude for the next coming customers, but don't do this in front of the customer because you can laugh, and it looks rude to the customer. Another trick is to think of something positive about the basics of the sales, or think about the numerous sales you have made before on your good days, but don't let the noes cast you down and affect your attitude because they can get on your nerves sometimes, but remember that the customer can say no today, but say yes tomorrow because not everyone can say yes today to buy your product and sometimes noes comes like a flood or like stones from the sky, you have to love to collect them still, I'm pleased to talk to customers and when they say "yes" those yeses are like milk and honey, the sweetest of all it's nice, so I like to work with "negatives" and yeses because they give me income and help me achieve my criteria.

Machine

So as a seller, you know no one and no one knows you, there is no friendship in business. You are a salesperson a machine that makes money and gives a product or service away in exchange for money, like a coke vending machine, but when you start to shy away because you are selling to your people or because someone is your relative or respected man or woman, then you lose, you fail, shyness is the enemy for sales and for the seller.

Handling Objections

Now, as a seller, you should be ready to accept any objection from the customer about buying your product. It's like football. As a striker or a team, the ball has to go through defenders to score goals, defenders are the objections a customer has to buy your product, and when you go through those defenders and respond to overcome those objections, scoring goals you can sell like popcorn, but if the objections cannot be overcome and dealt with, there is no possibility of scoring and winning the game. To be a good salesperson, you have to answer every objection the customer has. One day, as I went around selling my product, a group of colleagues were in a pub in the city near Trafalgar Square and I said, I'm offering my product for this amount, and one of them said, I don't have a CD-ROM drive anywhere. and I said, I can email you my music now, and he said, I don't have cash, and I said, I accept card payments, I have a card machine with me, and one of the women in the group said, Uh, do you want to work in sales Friend, you should join our company, you are superb, you have the answer to everything, so as a seller, you must answer all negative questions of the buyer that prevent the purchase of the product, and then reoffer the product to the customer, you will sell a lot.

Wow, Customers

As a salesperson, you have to impress your customers. You need to anticipate them by improving your business with the latest technology. In order for the customer to receive the product, if the customer says I'm paying with Apple Pay, you must have a payment method to receive the payment or a customer says to take an American Express credit card, you should be able to have it, if they want PayPal, you should be able to have it. You should have all these things, you should be the leader in this sales game.

Selling Is Like Acting

As a salesperson, you need to know that selling a product or service is like acting, you have to know how to trigger an action from customers, and speaking a certain way in a certain level of tone that will elicit a response from the customer when you make a presentation before you know it, 12 customers out of 2000 people you talk to will like and follow you because of your charisma and the way you provoke a reaction in them to follow you, like the great Hollywood actors who know how to control the reaction of the viewer to excite them to be followed and appreciated on the big screen, and they make millions. At the checkout (Box Office).

3 Reasons Why Customers Buy

There are three reasons why a customer buys from you. The number one reason is the interest in the product or service you are selling, so the customer must desire, like, or be emotionally moved to buy your product or service.

Second: the ability to pay. Customers must have the money to pay the price. You offer the product. So broke customers cannot buy even if they'd like. Your product because they don't have enough money. Third is the payment method, you need to provide all payment systems to take the customer's money, such as cash, card, PayPal, cryptocurrency, because some people pay in cash these days. Some people don't use cash, they pay by card or contactless. So if you're selling something and can only accept cash, you're losing customers because some customers can't buy what you're selling with a card, even if they'd like to, and even if they have the money to pay for it. So as a seller and as someone who wants to build a business, you need to make sure that you have all the payment methods available for the customer to buy. Contactless or card payments require a card vending machine. You also need to have PayPal, Stripe, and a wire that allows you to withdraw money online, Stripe, and other payment methods to successfully market your product and sell your services. As they say, you have to keep up with the times.

The Game Is About People

So, the lesson is to understand people and your customers. As a salesperson, people are the game, people are the field you play football on to win your sales. You have to understand every person you talk to, how they buy and how they refuse to buy because people are your game.

To play well and win the game, you need to understand the three types of customers you meet every day.

Campaigning for the Presidency

So, as a marketer, you need to make sure your product gets into everyone's hands, or through everyone's hands, before they decide, they have to read or hear the offer themselves and choose to say yes or no to your product. To give you money if it is a yes, and for them to take the product and return the product to you if it's a no. That's how it works, you sell, but you can't say you're selling something, and you don't talk to the whole world about your products. It is like a campaign for the presidency. You have to campaign in every community and across the country to get as many votes as possible to be elected president. Then you have to tell the complete world about your product. You have to tell everyone in the world one by one about your product and the services you offer, and when you reach the complete world, imagine if 1 million people will buy your product, that will make you a multimillionaire, it will give you everything, give you cars, a house to live as you will but sell, Sell, sell, talk, to everyone about your product or service without getting tired one person at a time, you will be fine. The definition of selling is: the activity of making products and services available to everyone so that people can buy them.

Paradise And Hell

So as a seller, sales are the same every day, sometimes you can sell less and sporadically, you can sell more, so you can make £60 on Monday, £70 on Tuesday, £60 on Wednesday, £50 on Thursday, £60 on Friday, £40 on Saturday but still meet your £300 weekly sales criteria, I always meet the criteria every week, so as a seller you have to know that not all days are the same, some days are heaven and some are hells on earth, but it still averages weekly, monthly, yearly sales, average income and sales plus profit and increase the growth of your business, so you have to understand that not every day is rosy, some days are tough, it could be the weather or changes in the economy like the COVID-19 pandemic. Or a country's recession or a change in seasons, but if you continue to work on the fundamentals of selling, you will see your sales business grow. You have to know your game, if you know your game, if you know your numbers, you will always win, so know your game as a seller.

Confidence as a Salesman

So selling is all about trust. To be a successful seller who can sell a product every day for an average of £60 a day to £300 a week, you need to believe in yourself, your product and your sales system. So, you have to trust the system to talk to as many people as possible every day. That's how you sell. If you don't believe in yourself, the system, and your product, then you can't sell because you're two-faced and thinking, oh, this is going to work, and maybe it's not. You don't know for sure, but if you are convinced, you will start talking to 2000 people a day with your product? To get your £60 and when you talk to 14,000 you will get £300 a week? You're a winner, and you're always going to win because you have confidence in the product and the system, so that's the key to selling. So, how do you gain confidence, you gain confidence when you test the system, and when you get results, it will build your confidence, and then you'll start to sell like it is second nature. It will be fun and interesting, and it will be like a game, a fun game, a joyful game, so you have to be sure that your products will sell because sales is a system, it's all about numbers? It's a numbers game, repeating a conversation with everyone by offering them your product at a price that equates to winning.

Written Salesman

Moreover, as a salesman, you are written, salesman, full body from head to toe, wearing a nice tie and nice suit, and you're looking a million pounds. You don't know anyone and no one knows you when it's time to sell. You are a money-making machine, you are a machine that talks to numbers that are people, you are a machine that collects 12 yes decisions out of 2000 people every day, and the noes don't bother you.

They are part of the game, they are part of the puzzle. Without noes, the game does not exist.

Listening to Customers Intently

Listen to your customer when the customer is in front of you, give the customer your full attention, full eye contact, full ear, hearing and full attention. If you don't listen to the customer, you won't be able to adequately meet the customer's needs to sell your product. The best salesperson is a salesperson who listens to the customer because by listening to the customer, you know exactly what they want, you know exactly if they want to buy, and you know exactly if they would rather not buy, and you know exactly if they will buy later, but if you're not paying attention, you're missing out on all of these things, so you will be constantly telling customers, do you want to buy this? And you will not be able to know the customer, so the best salesperson is the one who listens to the customer because if you listen to the customer, you will know your customer from the inside, and you will be able to look at the customer transparently.

The Mind of a Student

As a salesperson, you must have the mind of a student. You should always learn from the books. From successful people in this niche. If you don't study, you won't learn and discover new tricks and old tricks like what works and what doesn't in this game, if you don't have the mind to learn, you will fall behind and not be great. You will stagnate, you will be defeated, and you will fail because the world we live in is constantly evolving, so make sure that you have a student's mind to be, always in college, always in elementary school, no matter how much money you make or have made because in the sales game you can know 99%. But there's always that 1% you don't know.

A Game of Sales Is Like (Poker)

Selling is a game where you deal with 2000 numbers every day but roll all those numbers to find 12 lucky numbers of £5 each and if you multiply by 12 x £5 you get £60 and £60 x 7 = £420 a week, so you have to go through 14,000 figures a week, but one day the other 1988 numbers have different negative aspects, but you have to play more to get those 12 lucky numbers per day total 2000 Numbers.

The sales game involves selling 12 products per day and earning £60 per day, averaging £300 per week. So, you win, but if you earn less, you lose.

Lion Character

There's a common saying that women use when strangers approach them in public (I don't talk to strangers), but as a salesperson, you have to be brave because you have to strike up a conversation with strangers and approach them. And say, "My name is this, I'm selling this product. Do you want to trade?" It takes courage to sell to a person in groups because you are a nervous person, so it takes the audacity of a lion to attack because as a seller, you are on the offensive side and the customer on the defensive side.

Therefore, success in this game requires courage, the audacity of a lion.

Conversation

As a salesperson, your job is to find the conversation. As long as people can give you their attention, you're good to go because you need 20 seconds of their attention as a salesperson to pitch them your product and see if they're interested. 20 seconds of customer attention is all you need because if they're the right customer they can give you another 2 minutes then they can give you 4 more minutes, then they can give you hours, then they can give you a lifetime to talk to them. Therefore, when you approach a customer, you have 20 seconds of their attention to tell your short story or offer. Thereafter, if the customer wants your product, they will say yes and stay with you longer and longer. So, that's the customer's attention span customers give you as a stranger or a salesman when you approach them, and your speech must be suggestive and sweet, you must have a sweet mouth.

Things I Feel and Say to Myself Before Going to the Field

—I feel blessed before going out on the pitch

—I feel happy because I will sell and make money, that's why I'm excited

—I feel the joy of selling, meeting criteria and getting paid

—Today I will become richer and richer

—I know that I will make it, I feel it, I believe it, and the feelings of happiness and the joy of selling and getting rich start flooding me.

Selling Makes Rich

Selling will make you a mighty man, just like the mighty men of the earth. Rich men and women rule the country, they rule the world, they are powerful, strong, and celebrated. When you're rich, you can answer anything and solve any problem, as the Wolf of Wall Street said, "Deal with your problems by getting rich."

Chapter 8

Brains of a Salesman

Y ou have to have a salesperson's brain, you have to change your mindset and have a salesperson's brain, where you are trained and learn how to sell to make millions and billions on a £5 a piece product. Because if you sell millions, you have millions of pounds in the bank.

You Make the Rules

Selling is a game where you, the salesperson, make the rules to control your customer's mind. You can choose to manipulate the client, you have absolutely all the power and you determine the outcome of the game. You pick who wins and who loses, so you're both the judge and jury.

Ask a Question

So, how can I continue to market and sell my product to the same customers? If they have already bought it? I have seen from my experience that when you sell your product in the city, you start selling your product when no one knows about it and as time goes on as you're selling, everyone will know and get your product, so one day when I was selling and my customers told me that why don't you create and sell something new, like a t-shirt that goes with the music, because they already bought my Single music, that customer offer meant I had to create new songs that my customers are willing to buy, why keep bringing them the same old songs, so I'm wasting my time and opportunities. So, I have to sell t-shirts and hats as customers suggest and make a new album, and those who don't have my first music single can still have it. So, as a seller, you have to constantly improve the product and sell the product with new features. That's why McDonald's always comes with new menus and new technology, which encourages customers to keep buying the product because they know more is being added to the product to improve the user experience.

Every time, or a company like Apple is constantly adding new iPhone features and all its products, but it doesn't keep the same features forever because people have already bought those old products with the old features, so you can sell to the same people forever, Constantly improve the product, create new things. Facebook is also always adding new features to their website and Twitter is always adding new features and updating the design aspect of their website, which is how to market.

Distribution

The answer is that you need a vehicle called distribution and if the vehicle drives and distributes your product or service to every part of the country, every city, every community, every shopping street, makes you sales and makes you a billionaire, and you achieve your goal.

How Do You Sell?

For someone who has a product and wants to sell it, who wants the whole world to get your product in exchange for the price you set. Who wants to give your product away to 8 billion people on the planet? How can this happen? How to sell your product and get billions in return? The answer is, apply the sales fundamentals I learned in this book, and you will reach the top, to achieve your goals

Dinner Guest Speech

So, sales is like you giving a speech to 2,000 dinner guests sitting around dinner tables eating and drinking, you have to put on a dinner suit and deal with the guests listening to you, and 12 people will applaud you and give their money

As you continue your journey to become a millionaire, a billionaire, a trillionaire.

Game Time

When it's time to sell, I know it's time to play because now I'll collect my money from each of the 2,000 people I talk to every day. I'm full of excitement and a big smile on my face, and I talk to customers with milk and honey on my tongue, which is irresistible. At least 12 people will fall for my sweet tongue, they will bow down and give me money. To get rich and crown me king.

Every Job Is a Capital

It doesn't matter what kind of work you do, whether you get a job working in a supermarket, whether you're a cleaner or a street vendor selling large quantities, or you sell CDs, sell vegetables in the market, work in TopShop or JD, or work in a bank, the salary you get is the capital to save and start your own business. Once you have the capital, you can open and grow your own small shop and become a big player like any other entrepreneur, but unless you have the mind and wisdom to work for yourself and grow into a big company. Your bosses will forever pay you peanuts and make you their slave because you have no way to save money and start your own small business, you have no faith, and you don't know the way. You don't have the skills to achieve that kind of success, so the skill of selling is what makes people rich. With a skill to sell, you have gold in your hand, you don't have to beg for food! Knowing how to sell is a skill that makes you rich.

Old Man Gun to My Head (Joke)

As I passed through the customers, I approached an old man and said to him: I have a music single, and I'm selling it to everyone," he asked. "

"Is it jazz?" I responded,

No! It's happy music.

"No! I don't want it, I like jazz and I don't know what will happen if I take your, music whether it will make me happy or if it will make me point a gun to my head to shoot myself." That's when I started laughing at the part he said: "Or it will make me point a gun to my head."

Indifference

So, as a salesperson, never expect a sale during a sales conversation with the client. Always be in the middle. Don't be desperate, be Indifferent Always neutral and always let the customer decide yes or no, but if you expect a sale, the customer will leave you in the dark, you'll think "oh he'll buy" because of the positive response the customer shows you, but he or she won't buy at the end of the sales conversation and that refusal will destroy your attitude, so be indifferent.

Ambitious

To be a rich person selling a product or service, you have to be ambitious. If you are not looking to make a million, there is no way you will use the skills of a seller. If you don't aim to be a billionaire or trillionaire, you won't have the motivation or hard work to do whatever it takes to get there, so aim to make a million and become a millionaire, become a billionaire and aim to become the number one richest person, gain the whole world. Work hard to get there.

Be Ethical

When you succeed and achieve your goal, don't be greedy and take everything for yourself be ethical, being generous to your staff, the world, the homeless, the less fortunate, the widows, the orphans and this will ensure that you will always be more blessed than anyone else because you are ethical and everyone will like you and be happy for you, but if you keep all the money for yourself and abuse your employees, or destroying people and succeeding at the expense of others, you will not be ethical, you will make a rich business person that the world hates.

For example, Marcus Rashford's upcoming ethical battle for the provision of free meals in schools bears a striking resemblance to his own background of poverty. Despite his rise to the top of football, he continues to advocate for the rights of children, young females, and himself. In fact, he is currently the leading scorer for Manchester United, and his popularity among children and fans alike is electrifying. He is a truly generous gift to society.

Marcus Rashford MBE is an English professional footballer who plays as a forward for Premier League club Manchester United and the England national team.

Taking the Heat of Shame

Sporadically when customers don't want to buy, they will rudely dismiss you, but that's no reason to be offended, but you have to put up with the heat and still do the sales work knowing that it's all about the numbers, so move on to the next customer. As long as you finish selling 12 products on a given day it's like a boxing game. The best boxing fighter does a heat trap. The boxer takes all the knockouts from different opponents but still stands up to defeat his opponents and wins the fights at the end until he becomes the heavyweight champion. Despite the rough, Shame and disrespect, you still have to go through 2000 people to get your average of 12 sales a day.

Product Has to Pass Through the Numbers

Your product must go through the numbers. You have to pass 14,000 numbers, and you get a percentage from that. It has to go through a million numbers, a billion numbers, until it finishes reading all the billions of numbers on Earth, and when the process is complete, you make billions of money, making your product offering available to everyone.

You Need to Have Faith to Start A Business.

The business is for a businessman or businesswoman who believes that if I put 10,000 pounds as capital, I will get my 10,000 pounds back many times over, and I can expand the business to reach the whole world, so it is an entrepreneur's business. A seller starting a business, you have to be sure to start a business and raise your capital to start a business and market the business, you are not guaranteed that it will work, but you are guaranteed the laws that make the business work, so if you don't risk investing capital, you can't be successful, so you have to play your part. If you want to sell your product.

Chapter 9
Life Is Money

L ife is money. You cannot live a comfortable life without money. This is why many people are homeless. That's why people have problems because they don't have money. People struggle to pay their bills due to lack of money, life is money.

Learning to Sell Is Learning to Trade

Dealing requires experience and skill, and skill only comes through experience. When you master the skill, you understand how to be smart about getting what you want out of everyone's pocket because you know the way to win sales.

A Business Is Like a Fruit Tree or a Crop

You do everything in the farmer's process to grow crops, take some seeds, plant them, grow them, harvest them, get food, and trade the rest in a repeating circle, but you sow first. Without the necessary capital, you will never eat fruit from the business because a business is nothing but a fruit tree, or a crops growing in the field.

A Customer Question

The customer asked me, yes, you are offering me your product, but why should I buy your product? It was the customer's question: Is this my type of music? Do I want it? Will I have fun?

Will it make me feel happy? How will it help me? What will it bring me? So, as a seller, your product must be what the customer wants. It should answer the customer's questions. As long as the customer wants your product, and it can be useful to them, they will buy it, but if they are broke, they won't buy it, even if it can be useful to them.

Be Willing to Give a Refund to the Customer

If the product or service you provided to the customer doesn't work well, be prepared to take a loss and always make sure the customer is happy because if the customer comes to buy your product or service, and it doesn't work well, you tell them no, I won't give you a refund or fix the product for you because you used the product before, I want to avoid taking the loss as a business owner, then you fail as a business owner and that won't help your business grow, it won't expand you because you intend to keep a customer for life, you don't want a customer to come once and never again. Some business owners because they don't have knowledge, they don't look far. They are greedy. They are scammers, they will refuse to refund the customer they will refuse to repair the product to the customer's desired standard, causing them to lose their customers forever, and you will see that they will have a bad reputation as a company that does not refund customers their money when they are dissatisfied, and how low quality it is that company that sells those goods. This company will not be successful because it does not know business. Customer refunds, Customer satisfaction should be your number one priority so that the customer is always happy, even if it means your business loses some money, if the customer is for life, the customer will make up for your losses over time. By buying more products to get you rich, so don't be afraid to refund the customer, don't be afraid to exchange the product for the customer with a better product, and even if you incur a loss, don't be afraid because the customers will be happy, and we will definitely come back.

The Reason to Love the Noes

The reason you have to love the noes, no matter how much they come to you like raindrops is because without the noes you can't get the yeses, so you have to talk to noes for the yeses that will belong to you, therefore push until the yeses start coming because the noes push you to get the yeses until you get your sales averages, so noes and yeses are like directional road signs leading you to your final destination. As long as you follow the directions, you will reach your intended destination securely.

Coaching Is Very Important

Therefore, coaching is vital in this area of sales. You must read books to train you to play this game to paramount height. It's like any other game in life, Football players are good. They have talent, but they need a coach to train them, a healthy diet and a strategy to play football and win.

So, as a salesperson, you require a coach. In this book of mine, I teach people how to sell one product and how to sell 12 products a day, 72 products a week from scratch, and when they become a business, they can sell millions of products, billions of products with one product type Using this system, repeating the same thing you did when selling the first product, repeating the sales pitch, repeating the presentation, repeating the same smile, the same process, the same system, from one person to a million people to a billion people.

The Skill of Sales Acquired

The sales skills I have acquired will give me everything I want, money, houses, cars, private jets, yacht, and honor in society, and it will give me everything I want. I just have to keep selling, it's done for me.

Income Streams

You can't depend on one income stream because when one stream of income goes down when the day comes and something goes wrong, i.e. pandemic, floods, earthquakes with that one revenue stream, and you're stuck. You need to generate multiple streams of income to stay afloat and be comfortable that if one stream of income goes down. The next day, others will be working to cover you as a seller. Don't just sell one thing I sell different things like now I sell CDs, websites and write business books. Even if the CDs don't work, my books will make money If the sites don't make money, then the books will make money, so I will make money like a clock but as long as I depend on one income stream, when it stops, life stops and the battle goes on, so I learned a hard lesson that I need to create multiple streams of income to keep everything under control. And in business, we call it leverage.

Failing to Prepare

If you don't prepare, you are setting yourself up for failure because you have to prepare to succeed. The greatest woman in history, Oprah Winfrey, said that preparation is success. In one of her interviews, she said that preparation brought her success. This woman has interviewed people, big, and small in the world. She is one of the top female billionaires in the world, and this is my advice: if a salesperson wants to become famous in one day, go on the Oprah Winfrey show. And you will be known. After a day.

Watch Customer Make Decision

Your job as a salesperson is to effortlessly offer your customers your product or service and then watch them make a "yes" or "no" decision, period, you don't have to manipulate the customer or show signs of a desperate offer and let the sale be a surprise because sales are a surprise, you never know who's going to buy. Because the customer is not written on the forehead (buyer)

Attraction Versus Chasing for Sales

When it comes to sales, you don't go for sales, you attract sales as a sexy and beautiful woman who should not chase men, but she attracts men because of how beautiful and sexy she is or how she packs herself, wears nice colorful clothes, how she walks, so it's the same with sales, make your presentation sexy and attractive, make your product and packaging good and sexy, and customers will come in response to your offer or promotion.

Sell, Sell ,Sell

So as a seller, you sell, sell, sell until it makes you rich, until it makes you enough and more than enough. Learn how to market your product by following the process in this book, and you'll be fine.

Working

Work is food on the table, work is your clothes, work is everything, without work you can't afford life for yourself and your family, but fools spend their time sleeping, laughing and drinking, wasting time and at the end of the day, you see them begging for food and clothes. They don't even take care of themselves, they are in debt, they can't even buy a house, they don't even pay the rent they rely on the government benefit system, they will always complain, why? Because they are lazy and always ignore opportunities when they come, but hard work is the best thing that can happen to a man.

The Value You Provide

Therefore, for a customer to give you money, they want to know why they have to give you their money because they work hard for their money, they can't be just giving you money for nothing, you are not a charity? But you have to explain what your product or service will do for them, and how it will benefit them, and how it will change their lives for good. If they are satisfied with your product offer, they can buy it as a payment and reward for your work, so nothing in this life is for nothing you reap what you sow, if a farmer does not sow, he cannot reap.

Money Gives Birth to Money

The capital you put in, whether it's £5,000 or £10,000 or £10, to buy a product or service and resell it to people, and that money will add up as long as you tell people about your product, £10 will generate another

£10 until it becomes a million, billion and trillion as long as you let the sales system work on that product and service, talking to your numbers every day, playing the numbers game so that money makes money, like chickens and cows. Let them mate, and they will produce more. Like the saying goes, money makes money. How selling has changed my life for better. So now that I have all this sales knowledge, selling my product and going through the mind of the customer. I'm no longer homeless, I'm no longer begging. Now I know I've got a future, and now I've got a nice place to live on East Street, alongside old Kent Road. I live in a flat with

Picture of me standing my balcony facing the city of London

A bird's-eye view. I can see the walkie-talkie building, the whole city, central London, the whole elephant castle, the pickle tower, and the Canary wolf the Shard. I'm controlling my life now controlling how much income I want to make on any given day, week, month, and year. Now that I've discovered my talent as a writer, I need to keep working writing as many books as possible, even up to 2000 Business Books leaving behind me a legacy, to share this great secret I found, the secret of a customer's mind. That makes me happy. I love being an author, it's an exciting experience to give away my brain, gathering knowledge and pen thoughts down. Furthermore, I feel joy, so now I aspire to be alongside Shakespeare, to surpass him and leave a legacy as the greatest author that ever lived. Thanks for reading my book. I hope you have benefited from it.

Email: info@redlionofsales.com

Website: Redlionofsales.com

Tel: 07360159574

Mathias Machona Publishing

Flat 40 innis house east street SE 17 2JN

Email: info@redlionofsales.com

Tel: 07360159574